Everyday
RAW
Detox

To my lovely mom and sister, and to Matthew who helps
make many of my opportunities possible.

First Edition

16 15 14 13   5 4 3 2

Text © 2013 Meredith Baird with Matthew Kenney
Photographs © 2013 Adrian Mueller

Published by
Gibbs Smith
P.O. Box 667
Layton, Utah 84041
1.800.835.4993 orders
www.gibbs-smith.com

Designed by Drew Furlong

Gibbs Smith books are printed on paper produced from sus-
tainable PEFC-certified forest/controlled wood source. Learn
more at www.pefc.org.

Printed and bound in Hong Kong

Library of Congress Cataloging-in-Publication Data

Baird, Meredith.
  Everyday raw detox / Meredith Baird with Matthew Kenney ;
photographs by Adrian Mueller. — First edition.
    pages cm
  Includes index.
  ISBN 978-1-4236-3015-9
1. Raw foods—Therapeutic use. 2. Reducing diets—Recipes.
I. Kenney, Matthew. II. Title.
  RM237.5.B25 2013
  641.5'636—dc23
                        2012033056

Everyday
RAW
Detox

Meredith Baird with Matthew Kenney

Photography by Adrian Mueller

GIBBS SMITH
TO ENRICH AND INSPIRE HUMANKIND

Contents

Acknowledgments 6

Introduction
  Design Your Detox 7

Blended Fruit Tonics 15

Blended Green Tonics 29

Juice Tonics 41

Vegetable Tonics 53

Brewed Tonics 67

Breakfast & Dessert Tonics 79

Dips, Apps, & Wraps 89

Salad & Soup Tonics 101

Mains & Grains 117

Skin & Body Tonics 135

Resources 140

Index 141

Acknowledgments

I am very privileged to have an intensely supportive group of people surrounding me. Great friends and family equal extreme fortune. My life is a testament to serendipity. Following my passions has led me down the incredible path of making kindred spirits as friends, meeting the right people, and being able to do what I love. I have a job, without having a job, which is really a surreal experience. I feel incredibly grateful and blessed for all that I've been able to do thus far, and I look forward to continuing to bring healthy food and quality of life to as many people as possible. I truly believe that living a healthy life equals living a blessed life.

To name those of you specifically who have helped me and listened to me over the years: My mom and sister, obviously, as you have supported me through all of my "phases" and have both been extremely grounding and to my two dearest "raw foodie" friends, Jessica Acs and Simone Powers, you have made this book and many others possible. I owe a special acknowledgement to Simone for this book in particular. I couldn't have done it without her. Thank you to Amelie Arguindegui Mounetou who helped test many of these recipes, and is a very talented chef in her own right. And all of my other dear friends on the other end of the phone to lend a supporting ear—Greer Owings-Husserl, Cathy Buck, Suzanne Humphries, Jesse Harooni, Jasie Costigan, Kimberly Mahan, and Caleb Barr, and everyone who is a part of the Matthew Kenney team. And of course, to Matthew Kenney, my partner in life's adventures.

Introduction
Design Your Detox

Perfection Isn't Possible

You may have picked up this book in the hope of a prescription, as if I am going to inform you how to solve all of your problems by telling you what to eat. I'm not, because I don't know.

We are all completely different. How profound right? Not only is our individual genetic makeup completely different from each other, we all live in unique environments and have distinct lifestyles, habits, and desires. Detoxing isn't that simple. You can look at the obvious and start to eliminate processed and refined foods. You can take it to the next level and eliminate (or cut back on) animal products. You can read every book under the sun, study every herb on the planet, obsess about every morsel that goes into your body and it will still not eliminate toxins from your body. Why? Because there are a bazillion other factors out there that aren't under your control. The more you obsess, the more toxic you are. Having everything under control is the closest step to being completely out of control. Having things in balance and recognizing the ebbs and flows of emotions, environments, and routine is as close to the answer to wellness as I have. If you must eat something not in the queue of optimal health—enjoy it if possible and wake up the next morning and follow up with something healthier. Dietary perfection isn't possible. Perfection is the passion of control freaks. In a society where control is a commodity, we are constantly bombarded with the idea that we can be perfect. We look to gurus, leaders, and celebrities to tell us what to eat, how to live, how to look, and how to behave. The optimal diet—or perfection—is completely individual. Embrace your individuality and live your life in a way that makes you happy.

Savor the Experience

This is not said to be discouraging or to disregard the importance of nutrition. The food you eat has a huge effect on your health and happiness, and it is often under your control. When you make the conscious effort to put healthier foods into your body, you will notice a major difference in how you feel. Fresh, flavorful, beautiful, life-giving foods make you feel just that—more fresh and alive! It's no secret that we are essentially killing ourselves through our stomachs. Being bloated, lethargic, and stuffed with crappy food feels like crap. Not only is it not good for your physical wellness, it also blocks your creative energy and mental clarity. Really, who wants to feel that way? This energy that we get from food is not only from what foods we eat, it is also how we eat them. Eating is such an instinctual act; we forget that it is often one of life's greatest pleasures. It is a necessary pleasure! How delightful is that? How many other things qualify? Not many. Making a conscious effort to experience a meal in pleasure is just as important as what is on the plate. This means that you must be mindful. Dim the lights, eat with real utensils, chew your food, and SAVOR the experience. Have a glass of wine, and if you're saying no, drink your water or juice out of a real glass. Those people who are pounding smoothies in fluorescent lighting in front of their computers are completely missing something, and it is where the French and Italians get it right. Hovering your greens is gross, and gives you gas. Sip, relax, and enjoy!

This book is created to respect the fact that most of us don't have endless amounts of time for food preparation, or time to eat our food in the manner described above. It's not always realistic to get out the fork and knife, and even if it was, it's important to give your body the digestive break. These dishes are simple to prepare, and even if you are sipping your smoothie in your car on the way to work, breathe deeply, turn on good music, and enjoy. When you focus on the pleasure in the little things—the foods that you eat, the company you have, a moment of silence—then you have real health. Savor the moment. Cheers!

Live Your Lifestyle

The practical matter of detoxing your diet can seem completely overwhelming and the results usually last for one meal. Many get so fixated on an all-or-nothing approach that it makes food craving ten times worse and then they give up. Unfortunately, detoxing is usually nothing more than a crash diet that doesn't last. So now that we've lost the detox and lost the diet, what do we have? We are back at square one.

You may have noticed, but the new posh diet word is lifestyle. Living this lifestyle—that lifestyle—I'm a vegan, I'm a vegetarian, I do yoga . . . I'm a raw foodist! In order to be healthy you need to join some trendy cult, or have a lot of money. This doesn't have to be the case. There are people out there who don't necessarily want to join the lifestyle cult, but might actually be interested in healthier food as a viable, luxurious cuisine. We all want to be healthier. We all want to "detox" to some degree. We are also all human, therefore we aren't perfect and there will forever be an instinctual desire for the "forbidden fruit." Of course living a healthier lifestyle and incorporating more clean, healthy, and delicious foods into your diet is the goal. Eating an apple a day won't necessarily keep the doctor away. You should probably eat more than that, but eating more fruits and vegetables is irrefutably a good idea. It doesn't mean that you have to only eat fruits and vegetables.

Design Your Detox

Every recipe in this book provides a level of detox. Whether you want to cleanse for a day, a week, or just simply exchange one meal. These recipes are designed so that you don't have to do a complete lifestyle overhaul. Yes, these recipes are all raw, completely dairy free, vegan, gluten free, and free of refined sugars. Although we utilize nuts in some recipes, they are only used as garnish or to enhance a dish. None of these recipes are heavily nut based. The absence of dense nut bases and high sugar content is by design, not by compromise.

Other detox books may advise you to buy a new line of kitchen equipment. Relax. What you have in your kitchen right now will work fine. The beauty in much of raw food is the simplicity. Although there is a place for the gourmet, once you start incorporating more raw foods into your diet you will start to find satisfaction in some of the simplest dishes— an apple with raw almond butter, sliced avocado with sea salt and lemon, high quality lettuces drizzled with olive oil. It may sound so basic right now, but the cleaner your diet is, the cleaner the foods you start to prefer. However, since this is a cookbook, you'd probably be disappointed if I told you to just eat an apple with a few almonds. In order to make most of these recipes, I recommend three simple kitchen tools.

Juicer

For a reasonably priced, readily available option, we recommend the Breville Juice

Fountain. The Elite is our preferred model, but any of them work well. Breville is a sturdy machine that is easy to clean and looks good on your counter.

Blender

Vita-Mix and Blendtec are both excellent high speed blenders. They are an investment and not totally necessary for the majority of these recipes. If you need to choose between a juicer and a blender, choose the juicer. You can make most of these recipes work with a standard blender.

Tri-Blade Vegetable Spiral Slicer

This is an odd little garnishing tool. It can easily be purchased on Amazon and costs less than $50. It is a fun and easy piece of equipment to have around. Making vegetable noodle pasta is one of our favorite and super simple raw food dishes.

Why Raw Food?

We believe that raw food is one of the most pure, delicious forms of cuisine. Although every restaurant menu has a salad of some form, and most people DO eat some raw food every day, somehow the raw food movement got hooked on the lifestyle cult and missed the category of part of a balanced diet and a unique culinary expression. People enjoy all types of cuisine—Asian, Italian, French, Moroccan, and the list goes on, but for most people, raw food cuisine isn't on that list. Raw food is in fact a delicious part of a healthy, balanced diet. This cuisine is one of the most exciting, fascinating, and ultimately health giving ways to eat, and this book is intended to make that easier. Just like you might pick up a book on cupcakes and decide to bake some cupcakes, we hope that you will pick up this book and decide to make some recipes because they sound good (or interesting), will undoubtedly taste delicious, and will make you feel better.

Why Detox?

The battle between health and sickness exists constantly within us. By doing an occasional detox, you give your body a break from fighting the bad and allow it to be supported with the good. There are many reasons to detox—general health, specific minor issues, or chronic illness. Almost all illness is an expression of inflammation or immune deficiency—from the common cold, to skin issues, or even more serious diseases. They can all be connected. When you remove foods that are the primary causes of these inflammatory conditions and imbibe in nutrient dense foods, you are allowing your body to heal. You will be amazed at the internal healing process that can take place. All of these dishes support that healing process.

What Is Detox?

Detoxing is the process of removing all foods from your diet that can interfere with the natural healing of your body. When you eat a detoxifying diet, you remove the emotional and physical barriers of highly processed food, common allergens, and concentrated proteins. By removing these obstacles, you allow your body's internal healing mechanism to kick in. The recipes in this book are designed to supply your body with an infusion of vitamins, minerals, and antioxidants. When you focus your diet on whole plant-based foods you are giving yourself a little extra boost of health insurance.

Forbidden Fruit

Without getting too scientific, there are some basic principles of common allergy causing, inflammatory, and hyperimmune response foods. These foods should generally be avoided whenever possible. Although, you might not have an allergy, it is never a good idea to constantly tax your body with foods that are commonly hard on others. It is possible to develop a negative response over time. If you are constantly bombarding your body with yeasts, sugars, and acid forming foods luck might not stay with you forever. Even if you don't have a severe allergy, when you start removing these foods (or eating less of them), most people always feel better.

What Are Those Foods?

We recommend spending two weeks without any of the foods below. You don't have to avoid them forever, but try to leave them out for two weeks. We guarantee that you will feel the difference. If and when you reintroduce them into your diet, focus on quality and limit your portions.

The Wheat Feast

Once a health food, wheat is now a highly processed industrialized food. Most wheat currently available is poor quality and makes its way into the most unusual places. Vegan and vegetarian meat alternatives are almost always wheat. If you are eating a vegan diet with wheat-meat on wheat bread, consider that you are having yourself an imbalanced wheat feast. Although it may be cruelty free, this is not healthy, and it is cruel to your system. If you eat some wheat, we always recommend sprouted wheat, or suggest you use other grains like rye, barely, rice, or quinoa as an alternative.

Gluten Isn't Great

It may seem like everyone has a gluten allergy these days. The truth is most of us probably have some degree of gluten intolerance; our reaction might just not be as severe. Try filling up the baked good, cracker, and bread space with more fresh fruits and vegetables. We do not recommend replacing your gluten foods with sugar-laden, highly-processed gluten-free alternatives. That being said, just like wheat, all gluten isn't created equally. So if an artisan loaf of rye bread is on the table, a slice certainly isn't a crime, unless, of course, you have a severe gluten allergy. There are some nice gluten-free products available, just make sure to read labels and avoid ones with a lot of sugar. Less is always more when it comes to an ingredient list.

Dear Ole Dairy

Dairy isn't the devil, but dairy is an inflammatory food and very hard for many people to digest. About seventy-five percent of the world's population is genetically unable to properly digest milk and other dairy products. Lactose is common, and lactose intolerance is even more common. Industrialized cow's milk is a foreign food to our bodies. Although the USDA promotes dairy as beneficial in the fight against osteoporosis, the acidic quality and concentration of animal protein may actually contribute to bone loss. Cows' milk is one of the only foods that are specifically linked to acne. When you see that teenager with bad acne eating a sugar and dairy-laden ice cream cone, ask yourself which comes first, the chicken or the egg? If you eat dairy, goat or sheep products are always a better alternative. If you do choose to eat cows' milk, it should preferably be raw, and from grass fed, hormone and antibiotic free cattle. Fermented dairy is always better than milk or cream.

Coffee and Booze

We should all limit our caffeine and alcohol consumption. We love our tea or coffee, and a glass of wine at night is an essential luxury. Try going without for two weeks to break the addiction, and give your body a break. If you go back to it, limit to one small cup of each a day—a small cup equals 4 ounces. Why? Caffeine and alcohol are stimulants and they heighten immune response. For people with inflammatory diseases like arthritis, eczema, and psoriasis, stimulants increase your body's reaction and can make symptoms worse.

Garlic

None of our recipes contain garlic, onions, shallots, or other members of the allium family. Moderate consumption has very powerful anti-inflammatory benefit that has been shown to improve cardiovascular function, blood sugar balance, and aid in cancer prevention. Although they do have some recognizable benefit, we choose to exclude them completely.

This exclusion is due to the fact that alliums are classified in the rajasik—or energetic food category. This category also includes chocolate, caffeine, and alcohol. Alliums are powerfully stimulating to the system, and yet we foolishly consume them all the time. The same potency that gives them their health benefit, is also responsible for dulling the mind and the senses. Just like any other stimulant, garlic and onions should be treated with caution and consumed in moderation.

Sugar Isn't Sweet

Of all the foods on this list to avoid, processed sugar is probably the worst. Not only is sugar full of empty calories, it is addictive and ultimately unfulfilling so you tend to overeat it. Although empty calories are good to avoid, that is probably the least of sugars' evils. Sugar suppresses the immune system, promotes inflammation, increases cellular oxidation (makes you age faster), raises insulin levels, and promotes the growth of yeast which contributes to candida and other fungal issues. The list of alternative "healthy" sweeteners grows by the day—agave, coconut sugar, maple syrup, honey, and others. While all of these sugars have their place, and some nutritional benefit, we don't recommend eating them a lot. The safest sugar is from pure, fresh fruit.

The Golden Tickets

So now that you have read the bad list, what is on the good list?

Healthy Fat Is Where It's At

We are healthy fat freaks. If you lived through the 1980s, you may have spent a few too many years on the fat-is-bad bandwagon, so it's good to make up for lost time. If you want to "get the glow," healthy fat is where it's at. These healthy fats can be found in the plant-based form of nuts, seeds, avocados, olives, olive oil, and others. Good fats help nutrient absorption, cellular function, nerve transmission, and prevent inflammation along with many other bodily functions.

Amazing Antioxidants

We all know the word "antioxidant" but few of us may really understand what antioxidants do. Antioxidants are the weapons against cellular destruction and molecular oxidation. When cells in our body oxidize, they create free radicals. Free radicals expedite the aging process causing tissue degeneration, heart disease, diabetes, cancer, and more superficial problems like wrinkles. Antioxidants attack these free radicals and protect our cellular functions.

Magical Minerals

The issue and importance of minerals in our diet could fill another book. The modern diet is lacking in minerals because of the inorganic conditions that much of our food comes from. Historically, our diets were rich in minerals from the soil and earth. Now we eat highly processed food that is produced in highly manufactured conditions. Food-based minerals are the core nutritional value of the food we eat—from macrominerals such as potassium, magnesium, and calcium to trace minerals like copper, manganese, and selenium—they are all important. To increase your mineral consumption, make sure to buy organic, preferably local, and seasonal produce.

The Ten Detox Commandments

Although all of the recipes in this book are easy to make, recipes aren't all you need. There are some simple life skills that help you live and eat in a more pleasant and detoxifying way. I have said before, it isn't just what you eat; it is how you eat—and changing a few bad habits can be hugely beneficial.

1. **Water plus lemon.** Before you do anything in the morning, have a glass of filtered water with lemon. One lemon in one liter of water is a great way to get moving first thing (literally). This is the best thing that you can do for yourself. Sleep is very drying and the water with lemon is a powerful boost of hydration plus vitamin C. This is our number one routine.

2. **You're not a turkey.** Don't Stuff. People love to "stuff" themselves full. Full of greens or full of junk food—it doesn't matter. Don't stuff. When you stuff yourself you are stretching your stomach, your blood sugar gets out of whack, you torture your digestion, and you add stress to your body and lines to your face. If you are eating something heavy, eat less. Chew slowly, and savor. If you start practicing awareness when it comes to the quantity of food you eat, it will change your life. You may have heard the old advice, eat until eighty percent full. Well, you heard it again, eat until you are eighty percent full. Stuffing yourself full of healthy food won't make you healthy. Our idea of portions is terribly skewed. Please don't supersize me. Thanks.

3. **If you aren't hungry, don't eat.** One pet peeve is when people feel like they need to eat when they aren't hungry. If you aren't hungry, it is often your body's way of telling you "give me a break." Skipping a meal won't kill you. These mini fasts can be very beneficial to your health. Airplane travel and other nutritional wastelands are great places to eat less and drink more water. Of course we advise this within reason. If you are underweight or have a nutritional deficiency, consistent nutrition is very important. Please use good judgment.

4. **Move.** Yes, exercise is important. This doesn't mean that you have to go to boot camp seven days a week. Moderate exercise or just moving around more can make you feel so much better. Next time you are hungry, tired, and crabby—stretch up high and then bend over to touch your toes. You will feel a jolt of new energy.

5. **Don't eat fake food.** We could steal the phrase, "Eat Real Food, Mostly Plants" and ok . . . we will. This is the best advice. Substituting vegan this and gluten-free that is not detoxifying. Eating more fruits and vegetables is. Incorporating more fruits and vegetables into your diet is the key. Fake meat for real meat isn't necessarily healthy.

6. Use silverware. This might sound crazy as part of the Ten Detox Commandments, but it is true. When you eat with real silver, you tend to eat more slowly, thoughtfully, and carefully. Stabbing food with a flimsy plastic fork does not have the same mental satisfaction that eating with a proper service does. Eating with silverware also eliminates eating in the car, on the subway, while walking, and other various ways that we see people awkwardly eating.

7. Embrace the ritual. So much satisfaction comes from awareness. Being in the moment when you consume is important to health and happiness.

8. Don't eat if you have to go. Go where? To the bathroom. If you have to go to the bathroom while you eat, you cannot judge how full or satisfied you are. You will eat faster and uncomfortably. People actually do this.

9. Schedule snacks. Snacking within reason can be very helpful to maintaining a healthy diet. Becoming ravenous and overeating is definitely not healthy, but grazing all day long doesn't give your body time to digest or properly metabolize. It may seem ridiculously obvious, but keeping a few almonds or an apple around is a great balancing snack.

10. Take a seat. Take the time to sit down and eat your food. All of the above will be much easier if you take a seat.

Disclaimer

I am not a nutritionist, scientist, or medical doctor. My authority on this subject is solely based on personal experience and our own research. I do not believe that there is one answer for everyone. I do believe that introducing more whole fruits and vegetables into your diet is healthy. Processed foods can easily make their way into any diet—vegetarian, vegan, gluten free—it doesn't mean that it's nutritious. Even a raw food diet that is full of nuts, sugar, and dehydrated food is extreme in the negative direction. A whole foods diet is the key to a healthy lifestyle, no matter what your dietary inclination may be. The less processed the better. Unfortunately, in our fast-food, fast-paced society, many of us don't even know how to make a healthy meal, and especially don't know how to make them easily delicious.

My greatest talent is probably pleasure seeking, and I find it in the small things. Part of appreciating pleasure is finding balance. I eat a little chocolate every day, I drink a little wine almost every day, I drink tea every day, and I try to find healthy ways to savor moments. I don't believe in extremes (unless it is for an artistic expression) and all-or-nothing diets definitely aren't the answer. Finding pleasurable ways to incorporate healthy food into your diet is what this book is about. Design your detox and learn to savor the moments when you nourish yourself the best.

Blended Fruit Tonics

Blended fruit tonics are extra healthy fruit smoothies. This chapter's recipes are the training wheels to get accustomed to a cleaner diet. They are all simple to make and full of easy to find ingredients. Fruit smoothies are notoriously a false representation of health. They are typically full of fillers, sweeteners, and other unusual suspects. All of these recipes have an extra healthy boost and are free of any added sugars. If you prefer your smoothie sweeter, add one date or a few drops of stevia. Their natural sweetness and familiar flavor makes these recipes perfect for breakfast and kids.

Sweet Immunity

This combination might sound odd, but it is absolutely delicious. It tastes almost like sweet and sour candy. This smoothie is packed with vitamin C. The addition of a red bell pepper and cayenne make it high in capsaicin, which acts as a natural pain reliever and antibiotic. This smoothie is great for immunity and metabolism.

2 cups frozen strawberries

1 large red bell pepper, juiced

1 large apple, juiced

1 lemon, juiced

Pinch of cayenne

Blend all ingredients until smooth.

Serves 1–2

Banana Carrot Chai

This is an amazingly soothing smoothie—especially nice in the fall. If you don't have the patience to juice carrots, you can substitute extra milk and make a creamy banana chai.

2 frozen bananas

1 cup walnut milk (page 83)

1 cup carrot juice

1 teaspoon cinnamon

1 teaspoon vanilla extract

Pinch of sea salt

Blend all ingredients until smooth.

Serves 1–2

Blueberries and Cream "Kefir"

Blueberries are one of the most loved and highest antioxidant plant foods. Their powers include improving memory and stabilizing the nervous system. They are also low in calories and sugar. The addition of probiotics gives this easy to love smoothie an extra digestive boost. This is a great smoothie for kids before school.

2 cups fresh or frozen blueberries

1 banana

1½ cups nut milk of choice (page 83)

2 probiotic capsules

Blend all ingredients until smooth.

Serves 1–2

Pineapple Upside-Down Cake

This smoothie can be blended all together for a delicious pink smoothie or you can serve it in layers like we did for the photo just for fun. Either way it is uniquely delicious and nutritious. Pineapple is one of our favorite tropical fruits.

2 cups fresh or frozen pineapple chunks

1 cup frozen cherries

1/2 cup young coconut meat (optional)

1 1/2 cups coconut milk (page 86) or
   nut milk of choice (page 83)

1 (1-inch) chunk ginger, peeled

1 tablespoon coconut butter

1 teaspoon cinnamon

1 teaspoon vanilla extract

1/4 cup shredded coconut (optional)

Pinch of sea salt

Blend all ingredients until smooth.

To layer, blend half of the smoothie without cherries and half with them and then layer with shredded coconut.

Serves 1–2

Fall Fix

Juicing before blending is definitely an extra time-con-suming step, but if you have the time, it is worth it. In that respect, this smoothie is slightly more complicated than others, but don't let that turn you off. If you can find fresh-pressed apple juice, you can certainly use that as a substitution for the apple and the pear. This drink is best made in fall when apples and pears are fresh. The fall spices are soothing, warming, and beneficial to immunity and digestion. Honey is also a great immune booster during cold months. Almond butter and flax oil both add healthy fats and energizing properties.

2 apples, juiced

1 pear, juiced

1 (2-inch) chunk ginger, peeled

1 banana

1 tablespoon almond butter (optional)

1 tablespoon honey (optional)

1 tablespoon flax oil

Pinch of cinnamon

Pinch of cayenne

1 teaspoon vanilla extract (optional)

Pinch of sea salt

Blend all ingredients until smooth.

Serves 1–2

Skin Saver

Papaya is an amazingly rich source of enzymes, vitamins, and minerals. It is especially high in the enzyme papin, making it powerfully beneficial to digestion. Almond milk is rich in vitamin E, and flax oil is rich in omega fatty acids 3 and 6. This smoothie is truly internal skin food.

½ large papaya, approximately 2 cups

1 cup almond milk

1 tablespoon flax oil

Blend all ingredients until smooth.

Serves 1–2

Tummy Tamer

Guava is a tropical fruit that is popular in Asian countries. It isn't easy to find fresh, but if you live in a metropolitan city with a good Asian market, you can find it. Guava is known for being beneficial to all stomach aliments from diarrhea and dysentery to constipation. Guava is also soothing to coughs and colds. If you can't find guava, pineapple is a great substitute, although its tummy taming properties aren't as potent. You can use any coconut milk or nut milk, but Brazil nut is our favorite. We added probiotics to ensure good internal flora.

1 large guava, unpeeled and chopped, approximately
    2 cups (may substitute pineapple in equal amounts)

1 cup Brazil nut milk (page 83)

2 probiotic capsules

Pinch of nutmeg

Blend all ingredients until smooth.

Serves 1–2

Orange Creamsicle

One of my most loved mall foods when I was growing up in South Carolina was the Orange Julius. This smoothie is an attempt to recreate that drink without all of the crap. It is high in vitamin C and healthy fat from the coconut. The turmeric is an optional anti-inflammatory boost. This is a great smoothie in the morning because it is filling and very stable on the blood sugar.

2 oranges, peeled

1 cup young coconut meat

2 cups coconut water

1 tablespoon coconut butter

1 teaspoon turmeric (optional)

1 teaspoon vanilla extract

Pinch of sea salt

Blend all ingredients until smooth.

Serves 1–2

Tropical Pop

Vitamin C plus cayenne is the ultimate combination for boosting immunity and metabolism. Refreshingly tropical with the addition of mango, this smoothie is the perfect pick-me-up for a hot summer day.

2 cups fresh or frozen mango cubes

¼ cup yuzu juice (may substitute grapefruit juice) (optional)

1 cup grapefruit juice

1 lime, juiced

Pinch of cayenne

Blend all ingredients until smooth.

Serves 1–2

Raspberry Rhapsody

The flavor of raspberries and pineapple is one of our favorites—sweet, tangy, and delicious. The combination is full of vitamin C and antioxidants. It is enhanced with ginger for additional digestive fire.

1 cup fresh or frozen raspberries

1 cup fresh or frozen pineapple chunks

1½ cups water, coconut water, or nut milk of choice (page 83)

1 (1-inch) chunk ginger, peeled

Blend all ingredients until smooth.

Serves 1–2

Blended Green Tonics

The only thing scary about a blended green tonic is the color. A lot of people aren't comfortable drinking "green things." You will be shocked. These recipes are delicious. The fruit forward flavor of most of them makes it a sweet and efficient way to get your greens. If you don't have a juicer, blending greens is the first step to getting on the green bandwagon without a big investment. Once you get past the look, you will be hooked. One blended green drink a day is a great start to a detox routine. This chapter could be called "Get the Glow." We recommend adding your favorite greens powder or Vita-mineral Greens to any of the below recipes.

Pear-licious

This is one of our favorite green drinks. It is extremely cleansing and rich in beneficial healthy fat. We love pears, and they have less sugar than richer tropical fruits. This combination is delicate and the flavor is refined. Without the Vitamineral Green, it would make a great summer soup.

1 pear, peeled, seeded, and cubed

1 avocado, peeled and pitted

2 cups spinach

1 tablespoon coconut butter

1½ cups coconut water or nut milk of choice (page 83)

1 tablespoon Vitamineral Green (optional)

Pinch of sea salt

Blend all ingredients until smooth.

Serves 1–2

Coconut Cure

As a fair warning I will tell you that this drink tastes like classic Greek yogurt. The sour flavor may come as a surprise. If you don't like sour, add a few dates or a few drops of stevia to sweeten. This drink boasts all the health benefits of the coconut—healthy fat, fiber, vitamins, minerals, protein, potassium, and iron. The list goes on. Coconut also regulates hormones, fights infections, kills bacteria, and wards off wrinkles. Spirulina or green powder gives it an extra health kick. Hence the name, *Coconut Cure*.

2 cups coconut meat

1 cup coconut water

Juice of 2 limes

1 tablespoon coconut butter

1 teaspoon spirulina, Vitamineral Green,
  or blue-green algae (optional)

Pinch of nutmeg

Pinch of cinnamon

Pinch of sea salt

Blend all ingredients until smooth.

Serves 1–2

Clean and Lean

The melding of fennel and grapefruit is classic. Fennel has a unique combination of phytonutrients and anti-oxidants, giving it powerful anti-inflammatory and anti-cancer benefits. Fennel also aids in digestion and other stomach ailments. Fennel and grapefruit are both rich in vitamin C and beneficial to weight loss.

½ bulb fennel, chopped

½ grapefruit, peeled

1 tablespoon fresh mint, chopped

2 cups water, coconut water, or nut
   milk of choice (page 83)

1 date, pitted (optional)

Pinch of sea salt

½ avocado, peeled

Blend all ingredients except avocado until smooth. Add avocado and blend until creamy. Serve chilled.

Serves 1–2

Glorious Green

This is a classic green smoothie if you are new to the idea of blended greens. The flavor is surprisingly sweet and refreshing. This drink is packed full of health benefits—fiber, protein, vitamin C, antioxidants. It is extremely satisfying and makes the perfect start to a day!

2 cups frozen mango cubes

1 apple, cored and chopped

2 cups spinach

1½ cups nut milk of choice (page 83), coconut water, or water

Juice of 1 lime

1 teaspoon spirulina

1 tablespoon coconut butter (optional)

Pinch of sea salt

Blend all ingredients until smooth.

Serves 1–2

Great Grape

We had never really seen grapes in smoothies, so we had to try it. The flavor is, of course, delicious. Red grapes are rich in the flavonoid resveratrol, which is famously beneficial to heart health. Resveratrol is also a powerful anti-inflammatory and antiaging antioxidant.

1 frozen banana

1 cup frozen red grapes

1½ cups almond milk or nut milk of choice (page 83)

2 cups spinach

Juice of 1 lime

Pinch of sea salt

Blend all ingredients until smooth.

Serves 1–2

Tropical Greens

This is one of the most popular green smoothies at our restaurant. The combination of pineapple, coconut, spinach, and herbs is purifying and easy to love. Cilantro is one of our favorite herbs— it is very cleansing and high in vitamin K which supports blood and bone health. Pineapple is full of vitamin C and enzymes for digestion.

2 cups frozen pineapple chunks

1 cup frozen coconut meat or 1 frozen banana

1½ cups coconut water or filtered water

1 tablespoon coconut butter

½ large handful cilantro

1 cup spinach

Blend all ingredients until smooth.

Serves 1–2

Matcha Power

Matcha tea powder is the powerhouse of green teas. It is straight stone ground tea leaves, so you get the nutritional benefit of the entire plant. It is super high in antioxidants and is a great fat burner, cancer fighter, and energy booster. If you can't find matcha, it isn't necessary to make the drink, but you will lose a lot of the nutritional benefits. The coconut and avocado add extra healthy fat for glowing skin.

1 avocado, peeled and seeded

2 cups coconut water

2 tablespoon coconut butter

1 tablespoon matcha tea powder

Juice of 2 limes

1 teaspoon spirulina

1 date (optional)

1 vanilla bean (optional)

Pinch of sea salt

Blend all ingredients until smooth.

Serves 1–2

Magical Melon

This is the ultimate green drink for hydration. Cucumber and melons are both excellent for overall skin tone and health. The addition of spinach and herbs add protein, vitamins, and minerals. Because of the high water content, we recommend drinking this smoothie on an empty stomach or it could cause bloating.

1 honeydew melon, seeded, peeled, and
   cubed (frozen, optional)

1½ cups coconut water

1 cucumber, peeled and cubed

2 cups spinach

¼ cup mint leaves

¼ cup parsley

Juice of 1 lime

Pinch of sea salt

Blend all ingredients until smooth.

Serves 1–2

Miso Me-So Green

This is a savory green smoothie. Drinking a savory smoothie is an acquired taste, but once you get into it you will quickly recognize that it is incredibly satisfying. When I lived in Napa, I drank this smoothie every day for lunch.

1 avocado, peeled and pitted

1 large handful cilantro

1 cup spinach

Juice of 1 lime

1 red bell pepper, seeded, stemmed, and cut into pieces

1 tablespoon miso

Pinch of sea salt

Pinch of cayenne

1 cup water or unsweetened nut milk of choice (page 83),
   or more if needed

Blend all ingredients until smooth.

Serves 1–2

Juice Tonics

Juice tonics are exactly what the names says—healing combinations of fruit juices. Juicing is one of the easiest ways to incorporate more fresh fruit and vegetables into your diet. Juice is easily digestible so you assimilate the nutrients more efficiently. The antioxidants, minerals, and vitamins in juice are powerfully nourishing and healing to your system. All fruit juices are higher in sugar, and the lack of fiber in juice lets your body absorb the sugar more quickly, so we recommend limiting this category to one recipe per day as a meal replacement.

This chapter is really for making the transition to a healthy way of life. A big mistake that most people make when they start juicing is to drink too much fruit juice and throw their body sugar out of whack. In moderation, it is certainly very healthy and restores vibrancy and hydration to your skin. These recipes are enhanced with herbs and spices to make them extra healthful and to balance out the sugar. We prefer sweeter juices earlier in they day so that your body has a chance to metabolize the sugar before resting. Fruit juices should be considered a meal supplement, or drank only with small amounts of food for optimal digestion. Drinking fruit juice on top of a full meal is highly caloric and not conducive to detoxification.

Cranberry Cure

We all know that cranberries are good for healthy intestinal bacteria—especially for women. Cranberry also helps kill yeast overgrowth. Pear adds a light sweetness, and lime is the perfect balance of flavor. This is one of our personal favorites. It also makes a great cocktail mixer!

1 cup fresh or frozen (thawed) cranberries

1 pear

1 lime

Process all ingredients through juicer.

Serves 1–2

Spice-C

The combination of pineapple and orange is a mega dose of vitamin C, a powerful cold and flu fighter. Pineapple provides additional benefit with the enzyme bromelain which helps suppress coughs and loosen mucus. Jalapeños eliminate sinus congestion and reduce sinus headaches. Everything about this juice makes it a flu-fighter.

1 quarter fresh pineapple

1 orange

½ handful cilantro

½ small jalapeño, seeded

Process all ingredients through juicer.

Serves 1–2

Summer Heat

Watermelon is not only incredibly hydrating; it is also a powerful anti-inflammatory that is rich in lycopene. This juice is high in vitamins C and A and is rich in the minerals magnesium and potassium. The chili pepper boosts metabolism and fights infection. Low sugar, low calorie, and packed with nutrients—this is one of the most perfect detox drinks.

3 cups (1-inch) cubes watermelon

1 grapefruit

1 small red chili pepper

1 lime

Process all ingredients through juicer.

Serves 1–2

A Plus

This juice is an easy sell. It is a beautiful color, has a great flavor, and is amazing for you. Pineapple contains bromelain which acts as an anti-inflammatory as well as a digestive enzyme. It is rich in vitamins, antioxidants, and minerals. The addition of fresh turmeric gives a powerful anti-inflammatory boost. Because this juice is high in vitamin A and is powerfully anti-inflammatory, we give it an A plus.

4 large carrots

1 quarter large fresh pineapple, peeled

1 (1-inch) chunk fresh turmeric (optional),
   you can substitute 1 teaspoon dried

Process all ingredients through juicer.

Serves 1–2

Sun-kissed

Amazing for men and women! Apricots are rich in lycopene. Like tomatoes, they are good for prostate health. They are also high in magnesium, which improves bowel function and promotes relaxation, so this juice is great for menstrual cramps. Parsley and grapefruit provide a solid boost of vitamin C. If you can't find fresh apricots, you can substitute fresh peaches or other stone fruit.

1 fennel bulb, (including stems is
   optional for a more potent flavor)

½ large handful parsley

2 large fresh apricots, seeded (plums
   may be substituted)

1 whole grapefruit, peeled

Process all ingredients through juicer.

Serves 1–2

Minty Melon

Melons are one of the most hydrating fruits. They are high in electrolytes and enzymes which makes this a great post-workout drink. Papaya contains the enzyme papain, which is very beneficial to digestion, as is mint. The combination is refreshing, hydrating, and soothing.

¼ fresh large papaya, peeled, seeded, and cubed

½ fresh cantaloupe, peeled, seeded, and cubed

1 lemon

¼ cup mint leaves

Process all ingredients through juicer.

Serves 1–2

Melon Refresher

The best description of this juice is— super fresh! Light, refreshing, and packed full of antioxidants and vitamins, this juice is delicious. It is especially tasty in the summer when melons are at their best. Melons digest very quickly so it is important to consume this juice on an empty stomach or it could cause gas and bloating.

½ honeydew melon, peeled, seeded, and cubed

½ cup green grapes

½ cucumber

½ large handful parsley

Process all ingredients through juicer.

Serves 1–2

The Kiwi Key

Kiwis surpass bananas in their potassium content, making them the highest potassium-laden fruit. Potassium is one of the most important minerals, and is essential to maintaining good heath. Carrots and parsley add a substantial source of vitamin A and beta carotene. This is a very well-rounded, low-sugar juice.

2 kiwis, washed well

4 large carrots

½ handful parsley

1 lime

Process all ingredients through juicer.

Serves 1–2

Apple-aid

This is basically the Master Cleanse without the maple syrup. The combination of lemon, sweet, and spicy is wonderfully detoxifying. Think of it as spicy lemonade! This juice is a great way to alkalize first thing in the morning.

1 large apple

1 lemon

1 (1-inch) chunk ginger

Pinch of cayenne

Process apple, lemon, and ginger through juicer. Add cayenne to taste.

Serves 1–2

Berry Blend

Berries are a superfood. They are low in sugar and incredibly high in antioxidants, flavonoids, and phytochemicals. Berries are powerful weapons against free radicals. They are one of the highest antioxidant foods, making them full-body wellness warriors.

1 cup blueberries

1 cup blackberries

1 cup raspberries

1 cup strawberries

1 lemon

½ apple, if berries are not juicy

Process all ingredients through juicer.

Serves 1–2

Vegetable Tonics

Vegetable tonics serve the same purpose as juice tonics, without the sugar. Once you become more comfortable incorporating juice into your regime, we recommend consuming more vegetable tonics than fruit tonics. Most people become accustomed to the flavor of vegetable juices and start to prefer them to fruit. Green juice is so healing, nourishing, alkalizing, and refreshing. If you can take one thing from this book to add to your life each day, green juice is the best. Green juice is so powerfully packed with nutrients that you may even notice the color of your skin change to a light tan glow. We prefer it early afternoon as a pick-me-up before lunch. It is best to drink green juice at least thirty minutes before meal.

V10

You guessed it. V8 juice times 10. This juice is a complete meal, and totally satisfying. It also makes a great Bloody Mary.

4 Roma tomatoes

4 large carrots

1 small beet, washed and peeled

1 red bell pepper, seeded and stemmed

$\frac{1}{2}$ large bunch celery

4–5 leaves kale

1 large handful parsley

1 large handful cilantro

1 handful spinach

1 jalapeño, seeded and stemmed

1 lemon

1 lime

Pinch of cayenne, to taste

Pinch of sea salt

1 sprig rosemary

Process all ingredients except rosemary through a juicer. Garnish with rosemary sprig.

Serves 1–2

Clean Green

This is a light, easy, and clean green juice. Fennel is very warming and soothing to digestion. This juice is a nice combination for the fall or cooler months.

1 large fennel bulb
1 large bunch celery
½ handful parsley
1 lime

Process all ingredients through a juicer.

Serves 1–2

Breuss Juice Formula

The Austrian naturopathic doctor Rudolf Breuss developed this juice consisting of beets, carrots, celery, radish, and potatoes in specific ratios to provide a balance of basic elements required for the body's nourishment. This juice is used as part of a 42-day fast for total cancer treatment. The intended effect is to starve cancer cells. No matter what your intention, this is a balanced, powerfully detoxifying juice. We recommend this juice as an on-the-go lunch replacement. Using parsnip in the recipe really helps round the flavor, but it can be eliminated if you can't find fresh. We also use daikon radish in our recipe, but you can use 2–3 regular spring radishes if you can't find daikon.

1 medium beet, washed and peeled

1 large carrot

1 large parsnip

1 large celery stalk

½ organic russet potato, washed and peeled

1 cup sliced daikon radish

Process all ingredients through a juicer.

Serves 1–2

Sweet Cream

If you have never tried juicing a sweet potato you will be pleasantly surprised. The starch in the potato makes this drink lightly creamy, and the combination of sweet potato and carrot together is perfectly sweet. This is a dessert vegetable juice, packed full of vitamins A and B complex and beta carotene. Complete internal skin food! Yum.

1 large sweet potato, peeled

4 large carrots

1 lemon

1 (1-inch) chunk turmeric, or
   substitute 1 teaspoon dried

1 (1-inch) chunk ginger

Pinch of cinnamon

Pinch of nutmeg

Process all ingredients through a juicer.

Serves 1–2

Heart Beet

It is electric! This drink is super bright. Yellow beets make for a slightly less potent and more refreshing drink. Turmeric is a superfood spice—it is one of the most powerfully anti-inflammatory foods that you can consume. If you can't find yellow beets, you can certainly substitute red; you will just sacrifice the amazing color. Studies show that beets are beneficial in lowering blood cholesterol levels. The nitrates found in vegetables like beets help protect blood vessels.

1 large yellow beet, washed and peeled

1 large carrot

1 (1-inch) chunk turmeric, or
  substitute 1 teaspoon dried

1 lemon

2 tablespoons chopped fresh thyme leaves

Process all ingredients through a juicer.

Serves 1–2

Mediterranean

This juice is like a fresh tomato soup. It is light and refreshing. It is perfect for a hot summer day when tomatoes are at their best. This juice makes a great lunch replacement or an interesting starter to a meal if served as a chilled soup.

4 large plum tomatoes

1 fennel bulb

1 red bell pepper, seeds and stem removed

¼ cup fresh basil leaves

1 lemon

Pinch of cayenne

Process all ingredients except cayenne through a juicer. Add cayenne to juice before serving.

Serves 1–2

Great Green

This juice is light and refreshing, but extra nutritious with the addition of the vegetable powerhouse—kale. You can substitute spinach, chard, or any other dark leafy green for the kale.

½ large head kale

1 large bunch celery

2–3 limes (juice the limes whole for an extra tart juice)

Process all ingredients through a juicer.

Serves 1–2

The Classic

This juice is a classic, refreshing combination. The flavors and ingredients make it the perfect juice to have in the spring and summer when you can find all of these ingredients fresh.

1 large handful spinach (about 2 cups)

1 large cucumber

2 large carrots

1 small handful mint leaves, approximately ½ cup

1 lemon

Process all ingredients through a juicer.

Serves 1–2

Salad Spinner

Broccoli isn't juiced enough. Even though it is the quint-essential health food, it often gets left out of the juicer. Calorie for calorie, broccoli has almost as much calcium and is higher in protein than milk. Got Broccoli?

½ head romaine lettuce

1 large head broccoli

4 carrots

1 lemon

Process all ingredients through a juicer.

Serves 1–2

Herbal Infusion

Herbs are the most nutrient-dense food you can put in your juices. We always recommend adding fresh herbs to anything whenever possible. This juice is not for the faint of heart—it tastes super healthy because it is!

1 large handful parsley

1 large handful cilantro

1 cucumber

1 large bunch celery

1 lemon

Process all ingredients through a juicer.

Serves 1–2

Brewed Tonics

Some of these recipes are slightly more labor intensive than others, mainly because it might not be as easy to find all of the ingredients. Each recipe incorporates healing herbs or unique fermentation techniques for maximum detoxifying potential. Despite the effort it takes to make some of these beverages, they are the most medicinally healing combinations in this book. Herbs and brews are an important supplement to a detox diet. While all of the other chapters in this book are food—think of this chapter as medicine. These tonics also make a great alternative to wine and cocktails.

Coconut Kefir

Making your own fermented beverages can be a bit daunting and complicated, or at least I have always felt this way—especially if you don't know what the end result should be. Fear not! Coconut Kefir is insanely easy to make. It is much easier and faster than making your own kombucha (which has similar benefits). All you need to make delicious kefir are some fresh young Thai coconuts and water kefir grains which can be easily found on the Internet. When you make kefir with coconut water you have double benefit with the health properties of coconut water plus fermentation.

Kefir is a slightly sour, fizzy, probiotic beverage. It is the champagne of healthy beverages in both taste and nutritional benefit. The kefir grains convert the sugar in the coconut water to beneficial bacteria and microorganisms. Kefir helps restore intestinal flora and beneficial bacteria. Strong intestinal flora promotes strong immunity which is the key to optimal health. Kefir can help in the maintenance of candida, cancer, herpes, immune deficiency disorders, and digestive issues. Drink to your health!

4 cups coconut water (fresh is best,
  but you can use packaged)
¼ cup water kefir grains*

Pour coconut water into a glass jar. Add grains and stir with a nonmetal spatula. Place lid on jar and store in a dark, dry place. Allow to brew for 48 hours.

Pour kefir through a plastic sieve to strain. Store kefir in a glass jar at room temperature or in the refrigerator to keep chilled.

*Metal will damage the kefir grains. Do not use any metal when making your kefir.

Water kefir grains and milk kefir grains are essentially very similar, the only difference is that water kefir grains are vegan and more versatile.

Makes 1–4 servings

Blood Orange "Soda"

This recipe is beautiful with blood oranges, but if you can't find them, regular oranges work just fine. We juice the oranges whole with the skin. If you do this, use only organic. The combination of oranges, turmeric, and cayenne make this beverage an anti-inflammatory, immune-boosting, and mood-enhancing cocktail. Move over mimosa!

4 small to medium blood oranges

1 (2-inch) chunk turmeric, or 1 teaspoon dried

1 (1-inch) chunk ginger

1 teaspoon cayenne

1 liter sparkling water

A few drops of stevia (optional)

Juice oranges, turmeric, and ginger. Stir in cayenne. Add sparkling water and stevia, if using.

Serves 2–4

Chai Mate Latte

Chai is so tasty, but also super good for you. The herbal blend of chai is great for digestion and the spices are warming to the body. Authentic chai is used as a healing beverage in the practice of Ayurveda. This version is as close as it gets without the dairy and refined sugar.

Chai Tea Blend

2 tablespoons green cardamom pods

2 tablespoons tellicherry (black peppercorns)

1 tablespoon fennel seeds

½ teaspoon coriander seeds

½ teaspoon whole cloves

½ teaspoon nutmeg, coarsely grated

1 (4-inch) cinnamon stick, coarsely crushed

½ cup loose leaf mate leaves or rooibos
   or black Assam tea leaves

Stir all ingredients together.

Use approximately 2 teaspoons of mixture per cup of tea.

Milk

1 cup nut milk of choice (page 83), blended to froth

To serve, brew tea in hot water for 1–2 minutes depending on the strength that you prefer. Strain out tea leaves. Pour in milk and top with foam. Add honey or stevia if you prefer a slightly sweeter drink. Traditional chai is served very sweet.

Serves 2–4

Apple Ginger Water Kefir

If you don't have coconut water, or you don't want to make coconut water kefir, fruit kefir is also very easy and versatile. It is necessary to add cane sugar in order to ferment, but the kefir grain converts all of the sugar to healthy bacteria. The end result is not sweet. You can experiment with any dried fruit and flavors. Peach would be delicious to try in the summer!

4 cups water

1 (2-inch) chunk ginger

1/2 cup dried apple slices

2 tablespoon raisins

1/3 cup cane sugar

1/4 cup water kefir grains

Pour water into a glass jar. Add ginger, apple, raisins, and sugar. Stir well. Add grains and stir with a nonmetal spatula. Close lid and store in a dark, dry place. Allow to brew for 48 hours.

Pour kefir through a plastic sieve to strain fruit and grains. Remove the fruit from the cultures to stop fermentation. You can store the kefir grains in a small amount of kefir liquid in the refrigerator for up to a month. Store kefir in a glass jar at room temperature or in the refrigerator to keep chilled.

Note: Metal will damage the kefir grains. Do not use any metal when making kefir.

Makes 1–4 servings

Rose and Aloe Spritz

Rose is naturally soothing to the digestion and to the spirit. It is rich in antioxidants, and when combined with aloe, it makes a very elegant beverage to aid in digestion and skin health.

4 cups boiling water

2 tablespoons dried rose petals (found in your health food store, or dry your own from an organic garden)

Juice of 1 lemon

2 tablespoons honey or a few drops of stevia (optional)

1 liter sparkling water

2 tablespoons aloe juice

Gently stir rose petals into the water and add lemon and honey, if using. Allow to brew for at least 5 minutes then chill in the refrigerator. You can drink this mixture as a warm tea if you would like.

Once tea is chilled, strain rose petals. Add sparkling water and aloe juice and stir. Garnish each serving with brewed rose petals.

Serves 2–4

Vanilla Rooibos Tonic

This brew is packed full of vitamin C and antioxidants. Rooibos tea rivals green tea with its beneficial phytochemical properties. Cranberry juice rinses the body of the bacteria that contributes to the dreaded UTI. This drink is lightly sweet—perfect for a refreshing pick-me-up.

2 bags red rooibos tea or 3 teaspoons loose leaf rooibos tea

Juice of 1 lemon

1 teaspoon vanilla extract

2 tablespoons honey or a few drops of stevia (optional)

4 cups boiling water

1 cup cranberries, juiced

1 liter sparkling water

Add tea, lemon, vanilla, and honey to water. Allow to steep for about 5 minutes. Once tea is brewed, either remove tea bags or strain then chill. Once tea is chilled, add fresh cranberry juice and sparkling water.

Serves 2–4

Strawberries and Cream Tisane

Although not commonly used, strawberry leaf has a long history of medicinal benefits. Strawberry leaf is abundant in vitamins and minerals that are found to be beneficial during pregnancy. It is high in vitamin C, which helps absorb iron. Strawberry leaf is also a natural diuretic, which prevents water retention. It has been shown to aid in the healing of eczema and digestive disorders. In general, strawberry leaf is a mildly fruity herb that makes a delightful herbal infusion.

4 cups boiling water

2–4 tablespoons dried strawberry leaves

½ cup nut milk of choice (page 83) or coconut milk (page 86)

Honey or stevia, to taste

Pour boiling water over strawberry leaves. Allow to steep for approximately 10 minutes. Strain strawberry leaves. Stir in nut milk and add honey.

Serves 2–4

Green Grapefruit

Although all of the recipes in this book are beneficial to weight loss, this is the one that we can call the FAT BURNER. Green tea is famous for its fat burning effect, as is citrus fruit. The sweetener isn't necessary, but the honey really makes this drink delicious.

1 green tea bag

1 cup boiling water or warm nut milk of choice (page 83)

½ tablespoon honey or stevia

Juice of 1 grapefruit

Juice of 1 lemon

Juice of 1 lime

Brew green tea with water and honey for 1–2 minutes depending on the strength you prefer. Stir in citrus juices. Serve warm, or cold on ice.

Serves 1–2

Blueberry-Lavender Lemonade

This is the perfect summer lemonade—it is a favorite across the board. Blueberries give this drink a mega antioxidant boost, and lavender makes it extra soothing. In addition to being super healthy, don't be afraid to use it as a cocktail mixer!

3 cups boiling water

2 cups lavender flowers

3 cups cold water

2 cups lemon juice

1 cup agave, honey, or maple syrup
  (can be made unsweetened)

1 cup blueberries, muddled

Pour boiling water over lavender flowers and allow to steep for 10 minutes. Strain out lavender. Mix lavender water with cold water, lemon juice, and sweetener to make lavender lemonade.

To serve, add approximately 2 tablespoons muddled blueberries per 8-ounce glass. Top with ice. Pour in lavender lemonade. Serve with a glass straw.

Serves 4–6

Chamomile Nettle Tea

This is an old school brew for health and wellness. Chamomile is one of the most common herbs for relaxation. Nettles are packed with vitamins, minerals, and antihistamine and anti-inflammatory properties—making it great for immunity. Together they are detox warriors.

4 cups boiling water

1–2 teaspoons dried nettles

2 teaspoons dried chamomile

Honey or stevia, to taste

Pour boiling water over nettles and chamomile. Allow to steep for approximately 5 minutes. Strain chamomile and nettles before serving. Stir in honey, to taste.

Serves 2–4

Breakfast & Dessert Tonics

With this type of cuisine you can absolutely have dessert for breakfast and vise versa. What is better than dessert for breakfast? When you think about it, often these foods are in the same vein. Sweet foods are very soothing, and in moderation, very healthy. Natural sugars are an efficient source of complex carbohydrates. They are a natural energy source and are essential to the balance of the detoxification process.

Chia and Buckwheat Cereal

Chia is the new miracle seed. It has gained a lot of popularity in health food circles, and we think it is here to stay. Chia is rich in omega-3 fatty acids. It is a very stable seed, so it doesn't go rancid quickly. Unlike flax seeds, they don't need to be ground to make their nutrients available. This is an easy, simple breakfast. Feel free to add chopped fruit, spices, or nuts.

1 tablespoon chia seeds

1 tablespoon buckwheat

1 tablespoon pumpkin seeds

$1/2$ tablespoon hemp seeds

Pinch of sea salt

$1/2$ cup nut milk of choice (page 83)

Stir all ingredients together. Allow to soak for 20–30 minutes. Serve with fresh fruit and additional nut milk as a cereal.

Serves 1

Vanilla Nut Milk

Vanilla nut milk is the one thing out of this book that we make absolutely every day (or every other day). It is our favorite homemade kitchen staple. We like it with Brazil nuts the best, but try experimenting with almonds, hazelnuts, walnuts, and pecans. This milk is good with just about anything.

1 cup Brazil nuts

2 tablespoons coconut butter

4 cups water

2 dates, pitted (optional)

1 vanilla bean, scraped (optional)

Pinch of sea salt

Blend all ingredients until smooth. Strain milk through a fine sieve or nut-milk bag.

Makes 4 cups

Avocado Peppermint Ice Cream

If this makes it to the ice cream maker you are lucky. It is great straight out of the blender as a peppermint mousse.

5 medium avocados, peeled and pitted

1/2 cup coconut water

1/2 cup agave, coconut nectar, or honey*

2 tablespoons coconut butter

1 tablespoon peppermint extract

2 teaspoons vanilla extract

Pinch of salt

1/2 cup cacao nibs (optional)

Blend all ingredients until smooth. Stir in cacao nibs, if desired. Process through an ice cream maker according to manufacturer's directions.

*If you want to omit the sweetener, you can substitute 1/2 cup coconut water and add a few drops of stevia, to taste. This will make the texture icy, but it will still taste good.

Serves 4-6

Amaretto Millet

This bowl reminds me of cherry cobbler. Black cherries are sweet and delicious on their own. They are also rich in antioxidants and vitamin C. When fresh cherries are available, they are great in this recipe—if you have the patience to pit them.

1 cup cooked millet (page 119)

1 cup fresh or frozen and thawed black cherries

1 cup nut milk of choice (page 83)

1 tablespoon honey or a pinch of stevia, to taste (optional)

1 teaspoon cinnamon

1 teaspoon vanilla extract

1 teaspoon amaretto extract

Pinch of sea salt

Chopped walnuts, almonds, or hazelnuts (optional)

In a small saucepan on low heat, stir millet with remaining ingredients except nuts until all the flavors are combined. You will warm for approximately 2 minutes. Do not boil nut milk. The milk will make this dish creamy. If you prefer a dryer cereal, reduce the amount of milk. Serve with chopped nuts for garnish.

Serves 2

Cardamom Raisin Chia Pudding

If you've never had chia pudding, it is a must-try. Chia pudding has the texture of tapioca. We chose the cinnamon raisin version because it doubles as a delicious breakfast or dessert. Feel free to experiment with flavor combinations on your own.

⅔ cup chia seeds

2 cups nut milk of choice (page 83) or coconut milk (page 86)

¼ cup raisins, chopped

1 teaspoon cardamom

1 teaspoon cinnamon

1 teaspoon freshly grated ginger

1 teaspoon vanilla extract

Pinch of sea salt

Stir all ingredients together until thoroughly combined. Allow to soak in the refrigerator for at least 2 hours or overnight.

Makes approximately 6 servings

Coconut Quinoa

This recipe is sugar and fruit free with exception of a small amount of coconut. Getting accustomed to a less sweet breakfast is a great way to decrease sugar intake throughout the day. This bowl is full of satisfying protein. Ginger is great for boosting immunity and adding digestive fire. Turmeric is a powerful anti-inflammatory and gives this dish a beautiful yellow color, reminiscent of scrambled eggs. The coconut is a tropical addition that adds healthy fat and flavor complexity. If you want to add fruit, try fresh pineapple.

1 cup cooked quinoa (page 118)

1 teaspoon turmeric

1 teaspoon cinnamon

1 tablespoon freshly grated ginger

1 tablespoon coconut butter (optional)

¼ cup almonds, chopped

2 tablespoons shredded coconut

Pinch of sea salt

In a saucepan on low heat, warm all ingredients together for approximately 1 minute until the coconut butter has melted and the flavors are well combined.

Serves 2

Cinnamon-Scented Quinoa and Walnuts

Quinoa makes an amazing breakfast cereal. If you make too much for dinner, it is perfect as a leftover breakfast. Add whatever fruits and spices you like—this just happens to be a favorite combination of mine.

Cereal

1 cup cooked quinoa (page 118)

1 teaspoon cinnamon

½ cup walnuts, chopped

1 vanilla bean, scraped or 1 teaspoon vanilla extract (optional)

2 tablespoon raisins (optional)

½ tablespoon honey, or a pinch of stevia, to taste

Pinch of sea salt

Topping

½ cup nut milk of choice (page 83) (optional)

1 cup fresh fruit of choice (apple, pear, plum, banana, etc.)

Stir all cereal ingredients together. Top with nut milk and fresh fruit.

Serves 2

Creamy Coconut Milk

Try coconut milk if you are looking for a nut free milk, or if you just want a change of pace. This makes a great sweet treat after a meal!

2 cups shredded coconut, soaked in 4 cups warm water for 1–2 hours

1 tablespoon coconut butter

1 vanilla bean, scraped

2 dates, pitted (optional)

Pinch of sea salt

Blend all ingredients until smooth. Strain milk through a fine sieve or nut-milk bag.

Makes 4 cups

Mimosa Sorbet

This makes an elegant and clean finish to a dinner party, or try it with a few sprinkles of almonds and shredded coconut for a weekend breakfast.

1½ cups fresh orange juice (blood orange would also be good)

½ cup orange pulp

½ cup agave or coconut nectar

2 tablespoons coconut butter (optional)

2 tablespoons orange zest

2 cups chilled sparkling wine* (substitute coconut water, if desired)

Pinch of sea salt

Blend all ingredients except sparkling wine until smooth. Chill. Stir in sparkling wine until well combined. Process through an ice cream maker according to manufacturer's directions.

*The alcohol in the sparkling wine helps keep the ice cream soft after freezing. If you use coconut water it may get icy, but will still taste great!

Serves 2–4

Watermelon Ice with Avocado Mousse

This is a funky dish for a dinner party. It is easy to make and fun to eat. Hot pink and bright green screams fresh and the flavor holds up to its fresh look.

1 medium-size seedless watermelon

Avocado Mousse

3 avocados, peeled and pitted

½ cup lime juice

¼ cup agave or coconut nectar

1 teaspoon vanilla extract

Pinch of salt

Cut watermelon into 1-inch cubes. This should make about 2 dozen cubes. Freeze overnight.

Avocado Mousse: Blend all ingredients until smooth.

Assembly: Serve this dish fondue style with watermelon on skewers or with small forks, and the avocado mouse as a sweet dip. Alternatively, you can serve it plated with cubes of watermelon topped with small dollops of avocado mousse.

Serves 5–8

Dips, Apps, & Wraps

This chapter is fun. Who doesn't love a dip, app, or wrap? Appetizers and wraps are easy, delicious, and a great way to share your detox experience with others. We encourage you to get particularly creative with these recipes. We tend to make every eating experience a chance to wrap ingredients up and dip them. Although we haven't included a nori wrap, don't limit yourself—collards, Swiss chard, and nori are all some of our favorite vehicles for tasty fillings.

Collard Burrito

This is so good and so easy to make. Collards make one of the best wraps to stuff with just about anything. This is really best to make with leftover quinoa. You just toss all of the ingredients in. Good luck getting the filling to the wrap before you eat it!

4 collard leaves, stem removed*

Sunflower sprouts or sprouts of choice (optional)

Filling

2 cups cooked quinoa

1 tomato, diced

1/2 red bell pepper, diced

1/2 yellow bell pepper, diced

1/4 cup cilantro, minced

1 tablespoon cumin seeds

Juice of 1 lemon

2 tablespoons olive oil

1/4 teaspoon sea salt

1/4 teaspoon red pepper flakes

Pinch of cayenne

1 cup Avocado Crème Fraîche (page 99)

Filling: Toss all ingredients together except Avocado Crème Fraîche. Allow to marinate for approximately 10 minutes before serving. If you want to serve it warm, and you made fresh quinoa, toss ingredients together immediately and serve.

Assembly: Lay collard leaf flat and spread with a little Avocado Crème Fraîche. Fill with a generous serving of quinoa mixture. Top with sunflower sprouts, if using. Roll collard leaf tightly. Serve with extra crème fraîche for dipping. Slice in half, if preferred.

*You don't want to split the collard leaf in half. Just slice the stem out in a V shape.

Serves 4 large burritos or 8 small burritos

Curried Spinach Dip

Spinach dip is always an easy favorite. The addition of curry gives this an extra boost of health and flavor.

6 cups fresh spinach

1 large avocado or 2 small, peeled and pitted

Juice of 1 lime

2 tablespoons olive oil

1 tablespoon curry powder

$\frac{1}{4}$ teaspoon cayenne, more to taste

$\frac{1}{3}$ teaspoon ground cumin

1 date (optional)

Water, if needed to blend until smooth

Sea salt and pepper, to taste

Finely chop spinach and place in bowl of food processor. Add avocado and lime juice and blend until smooth. Add remaining ingredients and process until well combined. We love to serve this with standard crudités or jicama.

Serves 4–8 as a dip

Cauliflower Caviar

The beet chip makes such a delicious and simple chip; it is great for appetizers. You can use red or yellow beets, but the red will stain the cauliflower so it isn't ideal. This dish is tasty with leftover quinoa. Just substitute the quinoa for the cauliflower. Surprisingly it has a similar flavor and mouth feel to real caviar!

Beets

4 small yellow beets, peeled and sliced on
   mandolin approximately ¼-inch thick

1 teaspoon lemon juice

1 teaspoon olive oil

Cauliflower Caviar

1 medium head cauliflower, stemmed and chopped into florets

1 large cucumber, peeled and chopped

½ sheet nori, minced

1 tablespoon dulse

1 tablespoon wakame, soaked and drained

1 tablespoon olive oil

Juice of 1 lemon

½ tablespoon tamari

1 tablespoon agave (optional)

½ teaspoon coarse sea salt

¼ cup mint, finely minced

¼ cup cilantro

Pepper, to taste

Garnish

Micro mint (optional)

Beets—Toss beets with lemon juice and oil to preserve the color.

Cauliflower Caviar—Process all ingredients in the food processor until the texture is still slightly chunky and reminiscent of caviar.

Assembly—Drain beets if necessary. Lay beets out in individual slices on a serving tray. Place a few teaspoons of Cauliflower Caviar on top of each beet. Garnish with micro mint. For a variation, add a small scoop of Avocado Crème Fraîche (page 99) before topping with caviar.

Makes approximately 32 small bites

Seaweed Caviar Beet Chip, Avocado Crème Fraîche

This is one of the first raw food appetizers I came up with years ago to pair with champagne. Back then, I thought that it was brilliant. We have since seen various versions of this dish, but it is still equally delicious.

Beets

4 small red beets, peeled and sliced on mandolin approximately ¼-inch thick

1 teaspoon lemon juice

1 teaspoon olive oil

Hiziki

½ cup hiziki soaked with 1 cup water

1 tablespoon lemon juice

1 tablespoon tamari

½ tablespoon olive oil

Sea salt, to taste

Avocado Crème Fraîche

2 avocados, peeled and pitted

Juice of 1 lemon

1 tablespoon olive oil

½ tablespoon miso

Water, if needed to blend until smooth

Garnish

Micro greens

Sesame seeds

Beets—Toss beets with lemon juice and oil to preserve the color.

Hiziki—Rinse and drain hiziki. Toss with lemon juice, tamari, and sea salt.

Avocado Crème Fraîche—Blend all ingredients until smooth. Add water as needed.

Assembly—Drain beets if necessary. Lay beets out in individual slices on a serving tray. Place a small teaspoon scoop of Avocado Crème Fraîche on top of each beet. Top with another small teaspoon scoop of hiziki. Garnish with micro greens and sesame seeds.

Makes approximately 32 small bites

Ceviche Verde

When tomatillos are fresh, they are delicious. Try to find them at the farmers market in the summer. Smoky and savory, they taste a little bit like bacon. The milder acidity of this ceviche is very nice.

5 cups cremini mushrooms, stems removed and thinly sliced

1 avocado, peeled, pitted, and diced (2, if you prefer more avocado)

1/2 fennel bulb, thinly shaved

6–7 tomatillos, husks removed and chopped

Juice of 1 lemon

1 cup cilantro, chopped

1/4 cup olive oil

2 tablespoons finely minced jalapeño pepper, seeds and stems removed

Salt and pepper, to taste

Toss all ingredients until well combined. Allow to marinate at least 20 minutes before serving.

Serves 2–4 as a meal, 6–8 as an appetizer

White Mushroom Pâté

Mushrooms always make a satisfying substitution to meat. This pâté is equally delicious to its meaty counterpart. White mushrooms don't often get many health points, but they are a rich source of antioxidants and minerals.

3 cups white mushrooms, stems removed

1/4 cup sunflower seeds, soaked and drained

2 tablespoons white miso

2 tablespoons olive oil

Juice of 1 lemon

1 cup parsley, chopped

2 tablespoons fresh thyme

Sea salt and pepper, to taste

Process mushrooms, seeds, miso, oil, and lemon in the food processor until smooth. Stir in parsley and thyme. Salt and pepper, to taste. This is delicious served with crudités or sprouted grain crackers or toast.

Makes 3 cups or serves 16 as a small appetizer

Endive and Avocado with Cherry-Pistachio Relish

Endive is one of the most elegant vegetables. It is at its peak in the winter. When it's not in season, it can be expensive and hard to find. If you aren't able to get your hands on endive, you can substitute romaine, although the dish will be a bit clunky.

4 heads endive (about 16 equal-size leaves)

1 avocado, peeled, pitted, and diced

Relish

1 cup pistachios

½ cup dried cherries, unsweetened

2 tablespoon raisins (optional)

Juice of 1 lemon

½ cup fresh basil leaves

2 tablespoons olive oil

Sea salt and pepper, to taste

Relish—In a food processor, pulse all relish ingredients except salt and pepper until well combined but still chunky. Salt and pepper, to taste. Toss in diced avocado.

To serve—Place approximately 2 tablespoons of relish on each endive leaf.

Makes approximately 16

Sweet Pea Hummus

Peas aren't just for babies. They contain a unique assortment of health protecting phytonutrients and vitamins. Peas are a very balanced food rich in protein, starch, and healthy sugars. They are also considered to be one of the most environmentally friendly foods as they are nutritious for soil. If you can't find fresh peas you can use frozen.

2 cups peas (if frozen, thaw)

2 tablespoons tahini

1 tablespoon olive oil (optional)

Juice of 1 lemon

2 teaspoon cumin powder

Sea salt and pepper, to taste

Water, as needed to blend

Process all ingredients in a food processor until smooth. Add water as needed to make a smooth consistency. Serve this on a romaine leaf and top with sprouts for an easy hummus "wrap." Or serve with crudités as a dip.

Serves 4–8 as a dip

Avocado Crème Fraîche

Avocado Crème Fraîche is another staple in the raw food kitchen. It can substitute anything from ranch dressing to mayonnaise to sour cream. Adding fresh herbs is a great way to get creative.

3 avocados, peeled and pitted

Juice of 1 lemon

1 tablespoon olive oil

½ tablespoon miso

½ tablespoon apple cider vinegar

1 date (optional)

Water, if needed to blend until smooth

Sea salt, to taste

Blend all ingredients until smooth. Serve with crudité or vegetable chips.

Makes approximately 3 cups

Lettuce Cups with Stir "Fried" Shiitakes

This dish was inspired by the lettuce wraps at the chain restaurant P.F. Chang's. The original version is full of soy and uses iceberg lettuce. We upped the health factor by using butter lettuce and shiitakes. Shiitakes are one of the more medicinal mushrooms, with great immune boosting properties.

6–8 butter lettuce leaves, washed

Stir "Fry"

2 cups shiitakes, stemmed and diced

¼ cup diced carrots

¼ small jicama, diced

2 tablespoons tamari

1 tablespoon lemon juice or
   apple cider vinegar

1 tablespoon sesame oil

1 tablespoon freshly grated ginger

1 tablespoon agave (optional)

½ tablespoon sesame seeds

2 tablespoons chopped
   cashews (optional)

Toss all ingredients for the Stir "Fry" together. Allow to marinate at least 10 minutes before serving. If you have a dehydrator, you can marinate in the dehydrator for approximately 20 minutes to warm.

You can plate and portion the mixture in the lettuce cups, or serve as a dip.

Serves 3–8 as an appetizer

Salad & Soup Tonics

Soups and salads are always easy, delicious, and familiar. We have cleaned up and enhanced the norm by incorporating unique ingredients and blends. The art of salad making is truly a delightful skill. Salads are easy to share, and with the right mix of ingredients, they are completely satisfying. Soups are like a winter smoothie. They are packed with nutrition and easy to digest. It is important to get creative! Everyone has a different palate and preference. Don't be hesitant to experiment.

Asian Pear and Avocado Salad

The presentation of this salad can be elegant or rustic. We chose the elegant route, but it doesn't mean that you can't toss all of these ingredients together in a big bowl and make a delicious chopped salad. The creaminess of the avocado combined with the crisp pear is refreshing but decadent. Get creative with the garnishes and seeds, if you like.

1 tablespoon sesame oil

1 tablespoon pumpkin seed oil or olive oil

1 tablespoon grated ginger

Juice of 1 lemon

1 tablespoon black sesame seeds

1 Asian pear, cut into ¼-inch slices

1 avocado, peeled, pitted, and cut into ¼-inch slices

Micro greens (optional)

Whisk together oils, ginger, lemon juice, and sesame seeds to make vinaigrette.

To serve, alternate slices of avocado and pear on plate. Drizzle with vinaigrette and garnish with sesame seeds and micro greens.

Serves 1–2

Red Salad

This is inspired by one of the first raw food salads I ever experienced in a funky restaurant in Northern Florida. Shredded red beets and red cabbage are two of my favorite ultra health salad additions. Take it all the way to health food heaven with flax oil and cider vinegar. If you prefer a more mainstream flavor, olive oil and balsamic vinegar are also equally delicious.

Salad

1 red beet, peeled and grated on a mandolin

½ head red cabbage, thinly sliced

¼ cup mint leaves, minced

2 tablespoons flax oil or olive oil

1 tablespoon apple cider vinegar

Generous pinch of sea salt

¼ cup hiziki, soaked in ½ cup water for
   30 minutes and then drained

Curried Cashews

1 cup cashews

1 tablespoon olive oil

½ tablespoon curry powder

Pinch of cayenne

Pinch of sea salt

Salad—Toss beet, cabbage, mint, oil, vinegar, and salt and allow to marinate for 15 minutes. Add hiziki.

Curried Cashews—Toss cashews with oil, curry powder, cayenne, and salt.

Assembly—Toss salad with Curried Cashews. Ideally, allow to marinate 15 minutes before serving.

Serves 2–4

Rainbow Chopped Salad

This recipe is by no means exact. This idea can be applied to almost any variety of fruits, vegetables, seaweed, herbs, nuts, and seeds. Think of it as the ultimate bowl of nutrient-dense goodness. Just toss with a simple vinaigrette and you have an amazing meal.

1 large head romaine lettuce, cored and chopped

1 head red cabbage, thinly sliced

1 handful parsley, stemmed and finely chopped

¼ cup cilantro leaves, stemmed and finely chopped

1 apple, cored and chopped in cubes

1 Asian pear, cored and chopped in cubes

¼ cup wakame or hijiki soaked for 15 minutes, rinsed, and drained

1 sheet nori, cut into thin strips

2 tablespoons dulse flakes

½ head cauliflower, chopped into small florets

1 cup hazelnuts, coarsely chopped

1 cup pomegranate seeds (optional)

1 avocado, peeled, pitted, and sliced into cubes

½ cup dried apricots, finely diced

¼ cup sunflower seeds (optional)

3 tablespoons apple cider vinegar

2 tablespoons olive oil or hazelnut oil

¼ teaspoon sea salt

Pepper, to taste

Toss all ingredients together. Allow to marinate for at least 15 minutes before serving.

Serves 4–6

Winter Greens and Walnuts

This salad is a take on the classic massaged kale salad. We chose to take it in a more fall-like direction with the addition of thyme and walnuts, but you could certainly use any of your favorite herbs and nuts. Walnuts happen to be a favorite around here.

Salad

1 large head kale, stalks removed and thinly sliced

½ head Swiss chard, stalks removed and thinly sliced

1–2 tablespoons olive oil or walnut oil

1 tablespoon apple cider vinegar

1 lemon, juiced

Pinch of salt

1 apple (preferably gala), cored and chopped or shaved on mandolin

1 cup Inca berries or golden raisins, chopped

Walnuts

½ cup walnuts, coarsely chopped

2 tablespoons fresh thyme

½ tablespoon olive oil or walnut oil

¼ teaspoon sea salt

Freshly ground pepper, to taste

Salad—Massage kale and Swiss chard with olive oil, vinegar, lemon juice, and salt to break down the fibers. Once the salad is wilted, toss in apple and Inca berries.

Walnuts—Toss walnuts with thyme, oil, salt, and pepper.

Assembly—Toss walnuts with salad. Season with salt and pepper, to taste. Garnish with fresh thyme and walnuts, if desired.

Serves 4–6

Medicinal Miso

Miso is a fermented bean paste with a complex salty flavor. We love to use miso in many recipes to add roundness to flavor. Aside from having many culinary uses, miso is also a superfood. Miso contains all the essential amino acids, making it a complete protein. It is rich in B vitamins, including B-12. Miso is also rich in probiotics and aids in digestion. The medicinal quality of this soup is further enhanced with the addition of sea vegetables which are rich in protein and high quality minerals.

Stock

6 cups filtered water

¼ cup white miso

1 avocado, peeled and pitted
  (optional, to make a creamy soup)

1 tablespoon sesame oil

1 tablespoon dulse flakes

1 tablespoon grated ginger

Sea salt, to taste

Shiitakes

1 cup shiitakes, stemmed and thinly sliced

1 tablespoon olive oil

1 tablespoon nama shoyu

1 tablespoon lemon juice

Vegetables and Seaweed

¼ cup hijiki, soaked, rinsed, and drained

¼ cup wakame, soaked, rinsed, and drained

1 cup julienned carrots

1 cup julienned snap peas

½ cup thinly sliced radishes

Garnish (optional)

½ cup bean sprouts

Gamashio or sesame seeds

Stock—Blend all ingredients together until smooth.

Shiitakes—Marinate mushrooms with oil, nama shoyu, and lemon juice. Allow to marinate for at least 15 minutes.

Assembly—Before serving, stir shiitakes and vegetables into stock. If desired, garnish with bean sprouts and gamashio before serving.

Serves 4–6

Fennel and Zucchini Velouté with Tomato Seed "Caviar"

Dill is always a flavorful addition to any dish. Dill has a bright, sweet, and slightly tangy flavor that makes it very refreshing. Like many other spices, dill is rich in volatile oils that contain antibacterial qualities. Surprisingly, dill is also high in calcium. The combination of flavors in this soup is very Mediterranean. You could also forgo the caviar and drink this as a smoothie!

2 large fennel bulbs, juiced

1 lemon, juiced

2 cups peeled and chopped zucchini

2 tablespoons fresh dill

1 tablespoon olive oil

2 tablespoons miso

1 large avocado, peeled and pitted

Salt and freshly ground pepper, to taste

Tomato seed "caviar"

4–5 tablespoons of the interior of a fresh (preferably heirloom) tomato

Assembly—Blend fennel juice with all ingredients except for avocado until smooth. Add avocado and blend until creamy. Salt and pepper, to taste. Garnish with optional tomato seeds and additional fresh dill. Drizzle with a little olive oil and freshly ground pepper to finish.

Serves 2–4

Papaya "Poppy"

Papaya dressing is a take on the classic poppy seed dressing. Papaya is rich in digestive enzymes, antioxidants, and hydrating mineral properties. This salad is easy to like and super refreshing.

Dressing

1 cup chopped fresh papaya, reserve 3 tablespoons seeds

1 tablespoon dry mustard powder

½ cup lemon juice

½ cup lime juice

1½ teaspoons sea salt

1 cup olive oil

Salad

1 head Bibb lettuce, gently rinsed, stem removed, and torn into large pieces

1 tablespoon chopped tarragon

1 tablespoon chopped thyme

Salt and freshly ground pepper, to taste

Dressing—In a blender or food processor, blend the papaya, mustard powder, juices, and salt until smooth. With the motor running, add the oil in a stream and blend until the dressing is emulsified. Add the papaya seeds to the blender and blend until the seeds are finely ground

Assembly—Gently toss lettuce with dressing. Garnish with fresh herbs. Season with salt and pepper, if desired.

Serves 2–4

Carrot Mango Curry Soup

The color of this soup is magnificent. The combination of ingredients is powerfully detoxifying. Carrots are one of the richest sources of vitamin A and beta carotene. They are cleansing to the blood and the liver, making them nourishing for the skin. Ginger and turmeric are both potent anti-inflammatories. Curry, cayenne, and bell pepper all host an array of antioxidants and antibacterial properties.

Stock

½ pound carrots, approximately 4 cups carrot juice

1 yellow bell pepper

1 (1-inch) chunk ginger, peeled

1 (1-inch) chunk turmeric (optional), substitute 1 teaspoon dried

Soup

1 mango, peeled and pitted

1 tablespoon coconut butter

2 tablespoons miso

1 tablespoon curry powder

¼ teaspoon cayenne

Sea salt, to taste

Diced avocado (optional)

Stock—Juice carrots, bell pepper, ginger, and turmeric together.

Soup—Place juice stock with mango, coconut butter, miso, curry, and cayenne into a blender and blend until smooth. Season with salt. Garnish with diced avocado. Serve chilled, or slightly warmed in the blender

Serves 2–4

Fennel and Grapefruit Salad

Fennel and grapefruit make a classic, delicious, and nutritious combination. It also happens to be one of our favorites. This salad boasts many detoxifying properties. Fennel and thyme are both rich in volatile oil compounds that have antimicrobial and antibacterial properties. Thyme also protects and increases the absorption of healthy fats. Aside from its health benefits, this salad tastes like the Mediterranean. We eat it all winter.

1 fennel bulb, trimmed and thinly shaved on mandolin

1 grapefruit, peeled and cut into segments

2 cups arugula

1 tablespoon thyme

¼ cup cured olives, pitted and finely chopped

1 tablespoon olive oil

1 tablespoon lemon juice

Sea salt, to taste

Toss all ingredients together and allow to marinate for 15 minutes before serving.

Serves 2–4

Blood Orange-Scented Beet Soup

If you don't have blood oranges you can absolutely use regular ones, but blood oranges have an inexplicably delicious color and flavor that cannot be exactly replicated. This soup provides the full range of antioxidant, anti-inflammatory, and detoxification support.

Stock

2 large red beets, peeled

2 blood oranges, peeled

½ stalk celery

1 (1-inch) chunk ginger

¼ cup parsley

Soup

1 avocado, peeled, pitted, and diced (reserve a few tablespoons for garnish)

1 tablespoon olive oil

1 tablespoon miso

Pinch of salt

Pepper, to taste

Micro basil (optional)

Stock—Juice beets, blood oranges, celery, ginger, and parsley together.

Soup—Place stock juice with avocado, oil, miso, and salt in a blender and blend until smooth. If you want to serve the soup warm, blend for at least 1 minute. Season with pepper. Garnish with diced avocado and micro basil, if desired.

Serves 2–4

Mains & Grains

A detox diet is not a starvation diet. There is always a place for heartier fare. If juicing and blending aren't your thing, there is so much you can do with simply incorporating more complete raw food meals into your regime. These recipes make great meals to stand alone, or you can try them in addition to your normal meal preparations.

Think of these dishes as extra special salads. The technique of spiral slicing is an easy and inexpensive way to mimic the feeling of pasta without all of the refined flour and gluten. You can take almost any of the salad recipes and substitute the lettuce for spiral noodles—et voilà you have pasta! The same goes for the grains. You can add quinoa or millet to any salad to make it more filling. The addition of grains in the fall and winter can be very beneficial in cooler climates. All of these recipes are perfect served in beautiful bowls with a delicious glass of wine.

Quinoa

Although we consider and consume quinoa as a grain, it is actually a seed and therefore it is completely gluten free. Quinoa is one of the best sources of vegan protein, and because it contains all 8 of the essential amino acids, it is considered a complete protein. It is packed with a wide variety of vitamins and minerals and is high in fiber so it digests slowly and is filling and satisfying. Lower in fat than nuts, it is a dieter's dream.

Quinoa can be sprouted if you prefer to stay completely raw, however, we recommend cooking it. It is the perfect balance to a clean raw food diet, and gives a powerful boost of nutrition. In the case of quinoa, cooking it is good because you are enhancing the availability of the nutrients rather than depleting them.

How to cook quinoa

1 cup quinoa

1½ cups filtered water

Pinch of salt

Quinoa has a bitter coating, so it is best to rinse before cooking. Rinse, drain, and then place in water with salt in a 2-quart saucepan. Bring quinoa and water to a boil. Cover with a tight fitting lid, lower heat, and allow to simmer for 15 minutes. Drain and cool before serving. Quinoa should be fluffy and slightly chewy, but never crunchy. You can store leftovers in the refrigerator for up to 3 days.

Makes 3½–4 cups

Millet

Millet is another powerhouse and gluten-free seed/grain. Millet is extra special because it is one of the few grains that is alkalizing to the body. Millet digests much more easily than other grains, and it is hydrating to the colon which helps prevent constipation. Millet also acts as a probiotic, feeding the microflora in your intestine. It is also rich in fiber, vitamins, and minerals, and it is high in serotonin so it serves as mood enhancer! We love millet, and actually prefer it to most other grains.

The texture of millet varies greatly depending on how you cook it. If you cook it for a shorter period of time, the texture will be more like rice or quinoa; longer, it becomes slightly mushy and serves as a great substitution to mashed potatoes. You can use quinoa and millet interchangeably in these recipes. Millet is excellent with fruit and nut milk for breakfast.

How to cook millet

1 cup millet

2 cups boiling water

Pinch of salt

For a dryer, fluffy version: combine millet, boiling water, and salt in a saucepan. Immediately return water and millet to a boil. Reduce heat and cover the pan. Simmer until all the liquid has been absorbed, 20–25 minutes. Turn off heat and let stand, covered, for 5 minutes. Drain, and fluff with a fork. We prefer the dryer version for all savory recipes.

For a moister version: follow the directions above, but increase the water to 3 cups. Drain before serving. We prefer this version for sweet and breakfast applications.

Makes 3½–4 cups

Shaved Celery Root Linguini, Mushrooms, Truffle Pumpkin Seeds, and Sage

This dish is elegant, complex, and delicious. Celery root makes a great substitution for al dente pasta without all the white flour. We recommend tossing the mushrooms in immediately before serving because they will stain the color of the noodles.

Celery Root

1 large celery root, peeled and shaved with julienne attachment on mandolin

1 tablespoon lemon juice

1 tablespoon olive oil

1 teaspoon sea salt

Mushrooms

3 cups cremini mushrooms, thinly sliced

2 tablespoons tamari or nama shoyu

1 tablespoon olive oil

Truffle Pumpkin Seeds

1 cup pumpkin seeds

1 tablespoon truffle oil

1 teaspoon sea salt

Garnish

1 tablespoon minced sage

1 tablespoon minced parsley

Celery Root—Toss all ingredients until well combined. Allow to marinate for 10 minutes. Drain before tossing with remaining ingredients.

Mushrooms—Toss together all ingredients and allow to marinate for a few minutes.

Truffle Pumpkin Seeds—Toss together all ingredients.

Assembly—Toss celery root, mushrooms, and pumpkin seeds together. Allow to marinate for 10 minutes before serving. Garnish with extra pumpkin seeds and minced herbs. Drizzle with additional truffle oil before serving.

Serves 2–4

Beet Spaghettini with Pistachio Thyme Pesto

The beet "pasta" is always a fun surprise. We love the way this looks. Beets are rich in the phytonutrient belatin, which supports detoxification and is rich in antioxidants. Although the nutritional benefit is slightly different for yellow beets, they would also be a lovely presentation. Pistachios are buttery and delicious, but walnuts make a great substitution.

Beet Spaghettini

2–3 medium beets, peeled and processed through thin a spiral slicer attachment on a mandolin (should yield 8 cups)

Juice of 1/2 lemon

1 tablespoon olive oil

Pinch of sea salt

Pistachio Thyme Pesto

2 cups spinach

4–5 tablespoons thyme

1/4 cup olive oil

1/2 cup pistachios

3 tablespoons lemon juice

1 tablespoon nutritional yeast

1/2 teaspoon grated nutmeg

1/2 teaspoon sea salt

Pepper, to taste

Beet Spaghettini—Toss beets with lemon juice, oil, and salt. Allow to marinate while making pesto.

Pesto—Pulse all ingredients in food processor and blend until well combined but still slightly chunky.

Assembly—- Toss noodles with pesto. Garnish with chopped pistachios and a sprig of fresh thyme before serving.

Serves 2–4

Black Fall Quinoa with Radicchio, Shaved Fennel, and Cremini Mushrooms

We love radicchio in the winter. If you aren't familiar, radicchio is a dense leafy vegetable, relative to chicory. It has a sharp, bitter, and intense flavor that holds up well to dense foods like mushrooms. Radicchio is low in calories and rich in vitamins and minerals, including B complex and folic acid. High quality balsamic vinegar would also be really delicious with this dish.

1 cup black quinoa, cooked and drained

1 small head radicchio, chopped

1 small fennel bulb, thinly sliced or shaved on mandolin

2 tablespoons pine nuts

¼ cup fresh parsley, chopped

Juice of 1 lemon

2 tablespoons olive oil

1 teaspoon sea salt

Freshly ground pepper, to taste

Cremini Mushrooms

2 cups cremini mushrooms, thinly sliced

1 tablespoon tamari

½ tablespoon olive oil

Mushrooms—Marinate mushrooms with tamari and oil for approximately 10 minutes.

Assembly—While quinoa is still warm, toss all ingredients together. Allow to marinate for at least 10 minutes before serving so that the flavors can combine.

Serves 2–4

Millet with Avocado, Sea Vegetables, Vegetables, Sesame, and Mint

We could also call this dish a Buddha Bowl—a delicious, macrobiotic mix of flavors rich in iron, potassium, calcium, and protein. Millet, like quinoa, is actually a seed. It is nutrient dense and gluten free. If you simmer millet like we suggest in the recipe below it will have the texture of couscous, but if you add more water and cook longer, it will turn into a mash—more like polenta. Get creative with this recipe as it is by no means exact!

½ cup millet

1 cup water

Pinch of sea salt

1 tablespoon sesame oil

1 tablespoon apple cider vinegar

2 tablespoons black sesame seeds

1 avocado, peeled, pitted, and diced

¼ cup wakame, soaked and drained

¼ cup arame, soaked and drained

1 large carrot, julienned

1 cup shaved red cabbage

Tahini Sauce

¼ cup tahini

2 tablespoons lemon juice

½ cup water

Sea salt, to taste

Garnish

¼ cilantro

½ sheet nori, thinly sliced

Gamashio

Millet—In a small saucepan, bring the millet to a boil with water. Add salt. Allow to simmer for approximately 25 minutes. You want the millet to be fluffy, not mushy. Drain.

Tahini Sauce—Whisk together tahini, lemon juice, and water. Add salt.

Assembly—Toss millet with sesame oil, vinegar, and sesame seeds. Divide millet into bowls for serving. Arrange the remaining ingredients on top of millet. Drizzle with tahini sauce. Garnish with cilantro, nori, and gamashio.

Serves 2

Zucchini Noodles, Pine Nuts, Olives, and Tomato Relish

This is a more gourmet take on the classic "raw" zucchini pasta. This makes a great summery side dish or a light and satisfying entrée.

4 large zucchini, thinly sliced with flat blade of a
  mandolin (should yield about 8 cups)

1 teaspoon sea salt

Tomato Relish

3 cups chopped tomatoes (heirlooms if possible)

½ cup cured kalamata olives, pitted

2 tablespoons apple cider vinegar

2 dates, pitted

1 teaspoon cinnamon

1 teaspoon ground mustard

1 teaspoon ground turmeric

1 teaspoon sea salt

Garnish

¼ cup basil, julienned

¼ cup kalamata olives, pitted and chopped

Pine nuts (optional)

Shaved Zucchini—Toss zucchini with sea salt. Allow to marinate for at least 10 minutes. Drain and pat dry before tossing with sauce.

Tomato Relish—Pulse all ingredients in a food processor until well combined, but still slightly chunky.

Assembly—Toss noodles with relish. Garnish with fresh basil, chopped kalamata olives, and pine nuts, if desired.

Serves 2–4

Carrot Ribbon Pasta with Miso Tahini, Shiitakes, and Black Sesame Seeds

This recipe is so simple, delicious, and beautiful. Carrot ribbons are less watery than zucchini, so they hold up to sauce better and are easier to digest. Carrots are also one of the most detoxifying and nutrient rich vegetables.

Carrot Ribbons

4 large carrots, peeled and processed through spiral slicer (should yield about 8 cups)

1/2 head small red cabbage, shredded or thinly sliced

3 tablespoons black sesame seeds

Juice of 1/2 lemon

Pinch of sea salt

Shiitakes

3 cups shiitakes, thinly sliced

2 tablespoons tamari or nama shoyu

2 tablespoons lemon juice

Sesame Sauce

1/2 cup tahini

1/4 cup lemon juice

1 tablespoon miso

2 tablespoons sesame oil or olive oil

1 1/2 cups water

1/4 teaspoon sea salt

Garnish

1/4 cup cilantro leaves

Black sesame seeds

Carrot Ribbons—Toss carrots, cabbage, sesame seeds, lemon juice, and salt in a large bowl. Allow to marinate while making sauce.

Shiitakes—Toss shiitakes with tamari and lemon juice and allow to marinate for at least 10 minutes.

Sesame Sauce—Blend or whisk all ingredients until thoroughly combined and emulsified.

Assembly—Toss carrot ribbons and shiitakes with half of the sauce. Serve the additional sauce as a side for dipping. You can serve immediately or allow to marinate for 30 minutes. Garnish with cilantro and sesame seeds.

Serves 2–4

Quinoa with Cherries, Olives, Parsley, Avocado, and Lemon

Although most commonly considered a grain, quinoa is actually a seed relative of spinach and Swiss chard. We love to toss it in just about anything for an extra boost. This is one of our favorite quinoa bowls. Cherries, olives, parsley, and avocado are such a nutrient dense, delicious combination of flavors.

1 cup quinoa, cooked and drained

½ cup dried cherries, chopped

½ cup cured olives, pitted and chopped

½ cup fresh parsley, chopped

1 avocado, peeled, pitted, and sliced into cubes

Juice of 1 lemon

2 tablespoons olive oil

1 teaspoon sea salt

Freshly ground pepper, to taste

Assembly—While quinoa is still warm, toss all ingredients together. Allow to marinate for at least 10 minutes before serving so that the flavors combine.

Serves 2–4

Sweet Pea "Couscous," with Pistachios, Apricots, and Chili

Cauliflower "couscous" isn't for everyone. If you don't like cauliflower you can substitute jicama or parsnips. This dish is delicious in the spring with fresh peas, but you could take it in a more fall-like direction with mushrooms, apple, and warming spices. This recipe would make a great "stuffing" for Thanksgiving if you decided to get creative.

Couscous

2 large heads cauliflower

2 tablespoons olive oil

1 tablespoon miso

Salt and pepper, to taste

1 cup fresh or frozen peas (thawed and warmed under hot water if frozen)

1 cup pistachios, finely chopped

1/2 cup dried apricots (unsulfured), chopped

2 tablespoons minced mint leaves

1 tablespoon chili flakes

1 tablespoon orange zest

1 teaspoon ground cumin

Couscous—Pulse cauliflower, oil, and miso in a food processor until very fine. Season with salt and pepper.

Assembly—Toss couscous with remaining ingredients. Allow flavors to marinate at least 10 minutes before serving.

Serves 4–6

Buckwheat and Brussels Sprouts with Lemon and Pine Nuts

Buckwheat is beneficial in reducing cholesterol and lowering blood pressure. It is also rich in magnesium, which helps regulate blood flow. Raw Brussels sprouts aren't for everyone, but we encourage you to try them—you may prefer them over cooked! Brussels sprouts are nature's little cancer-prevention candy, full of detox supporting compounds. This dish definitely has an Eastern European flair, and tastes best in the fall and winter.

½ cup buckwheat

1 cup water

Pinch of sea salt

4 cups Brussels sprouts, trimmed and shaved on a mandolin

¼ cup pine nuts

Juice of 2 lemons

1 tablespoon lemon zest

1 tablespoon Dijon mustard (make sure it is dairy free)

2 tablespoons olive oil

½ teaspoon sea salt

Pepper, to taste

Buckwheat—In a small saucepan, bring the buckwheat to a boil with water. Add sea salt. Allow to simmer for approximately 20 minutes. You want the buckwheat to be fluffy, not mushy. Drain.

Assembly—Toss warm buckwheat with Brussels sprouts, pine nuts, lemon juice, zest, Dijon mustard, and oil. Add salt and pepper.

Serves 2–4

Broccoli Pesto and Quinoa "Risotto"

This isn't the most attractive dish, but it is oh so good! Broccoli is the ultimate super vegetable. Although you can make this dish with raw broccoli, lightly steaming it is actually beneficial to absorbing the nutrients, and in our opinion, makes this dish a bit tastier.

Broccoli Pesto

1 medium head broccoli, lightly steamed or raw

1/2 cup fresh basil

1/4 cup pine nuts

1/2 tablespoon red chili flakes

Juice of 1 lemon

1/4 cup olive oil

Quinoa

1 cup quinoa, cooked and drained

1/2 teaspoon sea salt

Pepper, to taste

Broccoli Pesto—Pulse broccoli in food processor to break into small florets. Add basil, pine nuts, and chili flakes. Pulse until well combined. Lastly, add lemon juice and oil and pulse until the oil is emulsified but the broccoli is still slightly chunky.

Assembly—Toss broccoli pesto with quinoa. Season with salt and pepper. To serve, garnish with a few pine nuts, basil leaves, and freshly ground pepper.

Serves 2–4

Skin & Body Tonics

The kitchen pharmacy is endlessly beneficial, applied both internally and externally. Sometimes you may find yourself looking like a crazy grandmother covered in remedies and potions, but they work! Body and skin care is often a case of K.I.S.S. (Keep It Simple, Stupid). Some of the best body products available contain no synthetic ingredients. Many of nature's most potent powers are really visible on the surface. As part of a detox diet, we recommend focusing on using as many natural products as possible.

Coconut Hair Mask

One of the most simple and versatile home remedies is coconut oil. You can use it for virtually everything—moisturizer, hair treatment, shaving cream, and make-up remover. Coconut oil is our number one skin and body tonic.

What?

Coconut oil—it is brilliant for anything hair and scalp related.

Why?

Coconut oil is high in lauric acid which is an antimicrobial and antifungal agent that protects the scalp from damage and bacteria that can cause hair loss, dandruff, seborrheic dermatitis, and psoriasis.

Coconut oil has a very high moisture retaining capacity. It is extremely stable and does not evaporate easily. Therefore, it is one of the best moisturizers for hair and skin.

Coconut oil is high in vitamin E which is a powerful antioxidant that is crucial to skin and hair health.

It is good for:
dry hair
frizzy hair
thinning hair
dry scalp
dandruff
seborrheic dermatitis
psoriasis

How?

Take a few tablespoons of coconut oil on the tips of your fingers and simply comb through your hair. If the scalp is your issue, make sure to massage it in the problem areas. Brush back hair and style as preferred. The oil melts to the touch, but is solid at room temperature. When it cools on your head it becomes instant hair gel without all the nasty, stinky, sticky crap. If you don't want to go out in public, do this treatment overnight.

You can leave the coconut oil in for a least a day. After your next hair wash you will instantly notice a huge difference. Your hair will feel much silkier, stronger, and smooth.

Castor Oil Body Wrap

Castor oil is a super high-density vegetable oil with a very mild odor and color. Because of its molecular density, castor oil absorbs very well into the skin making it an extremely effective moisturizer. It is a powerful anti-inflammatory and antifungal, so it is beneficial for various ailments, including abdominal cramps, headaches, muscle pains, inflammatory conditions, skin eruptions, lesions, and skin irritations. A castor oil pack is made by soaking a piece of flannel in castor oil then putting it on the area of complaint and placing a heat source, such as a hot water bottle, on top of the area. Castor oil packs are extremely powerful. Castor oil works from the outside in! The oil sinks through the epidermis and actually provides internal healing and detoxification effects. Castor oil is so powerful that it is said it can even induce labor.

Full Body Castor Oil Wrap (if you don't have a sauna)

Get the bathroom steamy hot with a little shower steam and a space heater.

Set up a pallet in the bathroom to relax.

Massage your whole body in castor oil (head included)—a little bit goes a long way.

Relax for 30 minutes.

Follow with a warm shower or Epsom salt bath.

Moisturize after the shower like normal.

This wrap is particularly good after drying flights and traveling. It is nourishing and detoxifying to the skin.

Vinegar Bath

Vinegar baths are used to restore the acid-alkaline balance in the body. Vinegar baths help prevent infection and are good in yeast regulation—possibly preventing yeast infections. Vinegar baths are also good for healing skin irritations like sunburn and other forms of skin inflammation. This bath is also especially good for the hair and scalp. Vinegar helps relieve dandruff and other scalp disorders.

2 cups apple cider vinegar

Add vinegar to a warm bath. Soak for no more than 20 minutes. After bath, rinse well and pat dry. Moisturize as normal.

Coffee and Sugar Body Scrub

Coffee is surprisingly good for external skin care. It is invigorating to the skin and helps with circulation, so it is good for the treatment or prevention of unwanted veins and circulatory problems. Sugar is good externally because it does not clog pores and it restores balance to the skin. If you want a finer grain sugar, you can pulse the coconut sugar in a spice grinder. Some people are more tolerant of a stronger exfoliator than others. If you have sensitive skin, definitely grind the sugar.

1 cup coffee grounds

½ cup coconut sugar (or sea salt)

½ cup coconut oil, melted

A few drops of essential oil (lavender is a favorite)

Mix all ingredients in a jar. This mixture can be stored in a cool place for about a week.

Use in the shower as you would a normal body scrub.

Salt and Sesame Oil Detox Bath

Bathing is one of the most detoxifying rituals. If you have dry skin, try giving yourself a warm sesame oil massage before getting in the bath to help retain moisture. Epsom salt helps ease stress, relieve pain, and helps in healing inflammatory skin disorders like eczema and psoriasis. Sesame oil is known as the "Queen of Oils." It has been used for thousands of years for skin care because of its natural antibacterial and healing properties. This combination is soothing, healing, and helps to moisturize the skin.

½ cup Epsom salts

½ cup sea salt

¼ cup sesame oil

A few drops of essential oil of choice, if desired

Add all ingredients to a warm bath. Soak for no more than 20 minutes. Make sure to relax and enjoy. After bath, pat dry and moisturize.

Avocado and Honey Face Mask

This is a classic and simple home remedy face mask. After you do this treatment, you will look like you've had a face-lift. Avocado is nourishing and moisturizing to the skin because of its rich fat and mineral content. Honey has long been used as a beauty treatment because of its ability to attract and retain moisture. The antibacterial properties in honey also make it a clean and safe home remedy to use.

½ avocado, peeled and pitted

2 teaspoons honey

1 teaspoon lemon juice (optional)

Mash avocado and honey together until smooth. Add lemon juice for skin lightening, if desired. Gently spread avocado over a clean face and neck. Allow to set for 15–20 minutes. Wash face with a mild cleanser and follow with your favorite moisturizer.

MSM Face Mist

The combination of herbs in this face mist is naturally moisturizing, soothing, and energizing. MSM is a naturally occurring form of sulfur with multiple skin benefits. MSM evens skin tone, and helps build and maintain collagen. Herbal face mist is an absolute must in the "get the glow" skin care routine!

1 cup distilled water

4 tablespoons chamomile tea leaves

2 tablespoons rose water

2 tablespoons aloe vera gel

1 drop lavender essential oil

1 teaspoon MSM powder

Warm the water. You don't need to boil if the water is already distilled. Add chamomile leaves to warm water and brew the leaves for 5–7 minutes. Strain out chamomile and allow the brew to cool. Stir in remaining ingredients. Place mixture in a spray bottle and always keep on hand for an instant, refreshing face lift.

Resources

Equipment

Blenders—Blendtec

There are other high-powered blenders available, but we like Blendtec because it is easy to clean and super efficient. www.blendtec.com

Juicers—Breville

Breville makes one of the most attractive at home juicers. There are many other juicers on the market, but Breville is "juicing friendly" and makes it easy. www.brevilleusa.com

Tri-Blade Spiralizer

This is a must have for most of the main dishes in this book. You can find them easily and inexpensively on www.amazon.com.

Ingredients

Now more than ever it is easy to find the ingredients and equipment to stock a raw food kitchen. Many supermarkets carry almost all of the ingredients in this book. Of course, we recommend doing most of your shopping at organic markets or co-ops and farmers markets, if they are available. For the harder to find ingredients, there are some great resources and brands that we support and recommend.

Navitas Naturals

For all superfoods and cacao products. www.navitasnaturals.com

Nutiva

For coconut and hemp products. www.nutiva.com

Earth Circle Organics

A variety of raw food products, including excellent sun-cured olives and sea vegetables. www.earthcircleorganics.com/products

Ironbound Island Seaweed

Sustainably harvested seaweed, and excellent quality dulse and other sea vegetables. www.ironboundisland.com

Cultures for Health

High quality kefir and kombucha cultures. They also stock fermentation crocks and other supplies. www.culturesforhealth.com

Index

A

A Plus, 48
Aloe Spritz, Rose and, 75
Amaretto Millet, 84
apples
 -aid, 51
 Fall Fix, 24
 Ginger Water Kefir, 74
 Glorious Green, 36
 Rainbow Chopped Salad, 107
 Sweet Immunity, 17
 Winter Greens and Walnuts, 109
Apple-aid, 51
Apple Ginger Water Kefir, 74
apricots
 Rainbow Chopped Salad, 107
 Sun-Kissed, 49
 Sweet Pea "Couscous," with
  Pistachios, Apricots, and Chili, 131
arugula, in Fennel and Grapefruit Salad,
 115
Asian Pear and Avocado Salad, 103
Avocado and Honey Face Mask, 139
Avocado Crème Fraîche, 99
Avocado Peppermint Ice Cream, 84
avocados
 Asian Pear and Avocado Salad, 103
 Blood Orange-Scented Beet Soup, 115
 Ceviche Verde, 97
 Clean and Lean, 35
 Crème Fraîche, 96, 99
 Curried Spinach Dip, 93
 Endive and, with Cherry-Pistachio
  Relish, 98
 Fennel and Zucchini Velouté, 112
 Matcha Power, 38
 Medicinal Miso, 111
 Millet with Avocado, Sea Vegetables,
  Vegetables, Sesame, and Mint, 127
 Miso Me-So Green, 39
 Pear-licious, 31
 Peppermint Ice Cream, 84
 Quinoa with Cherries, Olives, Parsley,
  Avocado, and Lemon, 130
 Rainbow Chopped Salad, 107
 Watermelon Ice with Avocado
  Mousse, 87

B

Banana Carrot Chai, 19
bananas
 Carrot Chai, 19
 Blueberries and Cream "Kefir," 21
 Fall Fix, 24
 Great Grape, 37
basil
 Broccoli Pesto and Quinoa "Risotto,"
  133
 Cherry-Pistachio Relish, 98
 Mediterranean, 63
beets
 Blood Orange-Scented Beet Soup, 115
 Breuss Juice Formula, 59
 Cauliflower Caviar, 95
 Heart Beet, 62
 Red Salad, 105
 Seaweed Caviar Beet Chip, 96
 Spaghettini, 123
 V10, 55
Beet Spaghettini with Pistachio Thyme
 Pesto, 123
bell peppers
 Carrot Mango Curry Soup, 114
 Collard Burrito, 91
 Mediterranean, 63
 Miso Me-So Green, 39
 Sweet Immunity, 17
 V10, 55
Berry Blend, 51
Black Fall Quinoa with Radicchio, Shaved
 Fennel, and Cremini Mushrooms, 125
blackberries, in Berry Blend, 51
Blood Orange "Soda," 71
Blood Orange-Scented Beet Soup, 115
blueberries, in Berry Blend, 51
Blueberries and Cream "Kefir," 21
Blueberry-Lavender Lemonade, 77
Breuss Juice Formula, 59
broccoli, in Salad Spinner, 65
Broccoli Pesto and Quinoa "Risotto," 133
Brussels Sprouts with Lemon and Pine
 Nuts, Buckwheat and, 132
Buckwheat and Brussels Sprouts with
 Lemon and Pine Nuts, 132
Buckwheat Cereal, Chia and, 81

C

cabbage
 Carrot Ribbon Pasta with Miso Tahini,
  Shiitakes, and Black Sesame
  Seeds, 129
 Millet with Avocado, Sea Vegetables,
  Vegetables, Sesame, and Mint, 127
 Rainbow Chopped Salad, 107

Red Salad, 105
cacao nibs, in Avocado Peppermint Ice
 Cream, 84
cantaloupe, in Minty Melon, 49
cardamom, in Chai Mate Latte, 73
Cardamom Raisin Chia Pudding, 85
Carrot Mango Curry Soup, 114
Carrot Ribbon Pasta with Miso Tahini,
 Shiitakes, and Black Sesame Seeds,
 129
carrots
 A Plus, 48
 Banana Carrot Chai, 19
 Breuss Juice Formula, 59
 Classic, 64
 Heart Beet, 62
 Kiwi Key, 50
 Mango Curry Soup, 114
 Medicinal Miso, 111
 Millet with Avocado, Sea Vegetables,
  Vegetables, Sesame, and Mint, 127
 Ribbon Pasta with Miso Tahini,
  Shiitakes, and Black Sesame
  Seeds, 129
 Salad Spinner, 65
 Stir "Fried" Shiitakes, 99
 Sweet Cream, 61
 V10, 55
Castor Oil Body Wrap, 137
cauliflower, in Sweet Pea "Couscous,"
 with Pistachios, Apricots, and Chili, 131
Cauliflower Caviar, 95
celery
 Blood Orange-Scented Beet Soup, 115
 Breuss Juice Formula, 59
 Clean Green, 57
 Great Green, 63
 Herbal Infusion, 65
 V10, 55
Celery Root Linguini, Mushrooms, Truffle
 Pumpkin Seeds, and Sage, 121
Ceviche Verde, 97
Chai Mate Latte, 73
Chamomile Nettle Tea, 77
Chia and Buckwheat Cereal, 81
chili pepper
 Ceviche Verde, 97
 Spice-C, 45
 Summer Heat, 47
 V10, 55
cherries
 Amaretto Millet, 84
 Pineapple Upside-Down Cake, 23

-Pistachio Relish, 98
Quinoa with Cherries, Olives, Parsley,
    Avocado, and Lemon, 130
cilantro
    Cauliflower Caviar, 95
    Ceviche Verde, 97
    Collard Burrito, 91
    Herbal Infusion, 65
    Miso Me-So Green, 39
    Rainbow Chopped Salad, 107
    Spice-C, 45
    Tropical Greens, 37
    V10, 55
Cinnamon-Scented Quinoa and
    Walnuts, 86
Classic, The, 64
Clean and Lean, 35
Clean Green, 57
coconut
    Cure, 33
    Creamy Coconut Milk, 86
    Orange Creamsicle, 26
    Pineapple Upside-Down Cake, 23
    Quinoa, 85
    Tropical Greens, 37
Coconut Cure, 33
Coconut Hair Mask, 136
Coconut Kefir, 69
coconut milk, 86
Coconut Quinoa, 85
Coffee and Sugar Body Scrub, 138
Collard Burrito, 91
cranberries, in Vanilla Rooibos Tonic, 75
Cranberry Cure, 43
Creamy Coconut Milk, 86
cucumber
    Cauliflower Caviar, 95
    Classic, 64
    Herbal Infusion, 65
    Magical Melon, 39
    Melon Refresher, 50
Curried Spinach Dip, 93
Curry Soup, Carrot Mango 114

D

daikon radish, in Breuss Juice Formula, 59
dill, in Fennel and Zucchini Velouté, 112
dulse
    Cauliflower Caviar, 95
    Medicinal Miso, 111
    Rainbow Chopped Salad, 107

E

Endive and Avocado with Cherry-
    Pistachio Relish, 98

F

Fall Fix, 24
fennel
    Black Fall Quinoa with Radicchio,
        Shaved Fennel, and Cremini
        Mushrooms, 125
    Ceviche Verde, 97
    Chai Mate Latte, 73
    Clean and Lean, 35
    Clean Green, 57
    and Grapefruit Salad, 115
    Mediterranean, 63
    Sun-Kissed, 49
    and Zucchini Velouté, 112
Fennel and Grapefruit Salad, 115
Fennel and Zucchini Velouté with
    Tomato Seed "Caviar," 112

G

ginger
    Apple Ginger Water Kefir, 74
    Apple-aid, 51
    Asian Pear and Avocado Salad, 103
    Blood Orange-Scented Beet Soup, 115
    Carrot Mango Curry Soup, 114
    Coconut Quinoa, 85
    Blood Orange "Soda," 71
    Fall Fix, 24
    Stir "Fried" Shiitakes, 99
    Medicinal Miso, 111
    Pineapple Upside-Down Cake, 23
    Raspberry Rhapsody, 27
    Sweet Cream, 61
Glorious Green, 36
grapefruit
    Clean and Lean, 35
    Fennel and Grapefruit Salad, 115
    Green Grapefruit, 76
    Summer Heat, 47
    Sun-Kissed, 49
    Tropical Pop, 27
grapes
    Great Grape, 37
    Melon Refresher, 50
Great Grape, 37
Great Green, 63
Green Grapefruit, 76
guava, in Tummy Tamer, 25

H

Heart Beet, 62
Herbal Infusion, 65
hiziki
    Medicinal Miso, 111

Rainbow Chopped Salad, 107
Red Salad, 105
Seaweed Caviar Beet Chip, 96
honeydew melon
    Magical Melon, 39
    Melon Refresher, 50

I

Inca berries, in Winter Greens and
    Walnuts, 109

J

jicama, in Stir "Fried" Shiitakes, 99

K

kale
    Great Green, 63
    V10, 55
    Winter Greens and Walnuts, 109
kefir grains
    Apple Ginger Water Kefir, 74
    Coconut Kefir, 69
Kiwi Key, The, 50

L

Lavender Lemonade, Blueberry-, 77
lemons
    Apple-aid, 51
    Blueberry-Lavender Lemonade, 77
    Buckwheat and Brussels Sprouts
        with Lemon and Pine Nuts, 132
    Quinoa with Cherries, Olives, Parsley,
        Avocado, and Lemon, 130
    with water, 12
lettuce
    Cups with Stir "Fried" Shiitakes, 99
    Papaya "Poppy," 113
    Rainbow Chopped Salad, 107
    Salad Spinner, 65
Lettuce Cups with Stir "Fried" Shiitakes, 99
limes
    Coconut Cure, 33
    Great Green, 63
    Matcha Power, 38

M

MSM Face Mist, 139
Magical Melon, 39
mango
    Carrot, Curry Soup, 114
    Glorious Green, 36
    Tropical Pop, 27
Matcha Power, 38

Mate Latte, Chai, 73
Medicinal Miso, 111
Mediterranean, 63
Melon Refresher, 50
millet, 119
Millet, Amaretto 84
Millet with Avocado, Sea Vegetables,
    Vegetables, Sesame, and Mint, 127
Mimosa Sorbet, 87
mint
    Cauliflower Caviar, 95
    Classic, 64
    Clean and Lean, 35
    Magical Melon, 39
    Minty Melon, 49
    Red Salad, 105
    Sweet Pea "Couscous," with
        Pistachios, Apricots, and Chili, 131
Minty Melon, 49
miso
    Blood Orange-Scented Beet Soup, 115
    Carrot Mango Curry Soup, 114
    Carrot Ribbon Pasta with Miso Tahini,
        Shiitakes, and Black Sesame
        Seeds, 129
    Sweet Pea "Couscous," with
        Pistachios, Apricots, and Chili, 131
    Fennel and Zucchini Velouté, 112
    Me-So Green, 39
    Medicinal Miso, 111
    White Mushroom Pâté, 97
Miso Me-So Green, 39
mushrooms
    Black Fall Quinoa with Radicchio,
        Shaved Fennel, and Cremini
        Mushrooms, 125
    Carrot Ribbon Pasta with Miso Tahini,
        Shiitakes, and Black Sesame
        Seeds, 129
    Ceviche Verde, 97
    Medicinal Miso, 111
    Shaved Celery Root Linguini,
        Mushrooms, Truffle Pumpkin
        Seeds, and Sage, 121
    Stir "Fried" Shiitakes, 99
    White Mushroom Pâté, 97

N

Nettle Tea, Chamomile, 77
nut milk, 83
nuts
    Cherry-Pistachio Relish, 98
    Cinnamon-Scented Quinoa and
        Walnuts, 86
    Coconut Quinoa, 85

Pistachio Thyme Pesto, 123
Rainbow Chopped Salad, 107
Red Salad, 105
Stir "Fried" Shiitakes, 99
Sweet Pea "Couscous," with
    Pistachios, Apricots, and Chili, 131
Winter Greens and Walnuts, 109

O

olives
    Fennel and Grapefruit Salad, 115
    Quinoa with Cherries, Olives, Parsley,
        Avocado, and Lemon, 130
    Zucchini Noodles, Pine Nuts, Olives,
        and Tomato Relish, 128
Orange Creamsicle, 26
oranges
    Blood Orange-Scented Beet Soup, 115
    Blood Orange "Soda," 71
    Creamsicle, 26
    Mimosa Sorbet, 87
    Spice-C, 45

P

papaya
    Minty Melon, 49
    "Poppy," 113
    Skin Saver, 25
Papaya "Poppy," 113
parsley
    Black Fall Quinoa with Radicchio,
        Shaved Fennel, and Cremini
        Mushrooms, 125
    Blood Orange-Scented Beet Soup, 115
    Clean Green, 57
    Herbal Infusion, 65
    Kiwi Key, 50
    Magical Melon, 39
    Melon Refresher, 50
    Quinoa with Cherries, Olives, Parsley,
        Avocado, and Lemon, 130
    Rainbow Chopped Salad, 107
    Sun-Kissed, 49
    V10, 55
    White Mushroom Pâté, 97
parsnips, in Breuss Juice Formula, 59
Pear-licious, 31
pears
    Asian, and Avocado Salad, 103
    Cranberry Cure, 43
    Fall Fix, 24
    Pear-licious, 31
    Rainbow Chopped Salad, 107
peas
    Medicinal Miso, 111

Sweet Pea "Couscous," with
    Pistachios, Apricots, and Chili, 131
Sweet Pea Hummus, 98
peppercorns, in Chai Mate Latte, 73
pineapple
    A Plus, 48
    Raspberry Rhapsody, 27
    Spice-C, 45
    Tropical Greens, 37
    Upside-Down Cake, 23
Pineapple Upside-Down Cake, 23
pine nuts
    Black Fall Quinoa with Radicchio,
        Shaved Fennel, and Cremini
        Mushrooms, 125
    Broccoli Pesto and Quinoa "Risotto,"
        133
    Buckwheat and Brussels Sprouts
        with Lemon and Pine Nuts, 132
    Zucchini Noodles, Pine Nuts, Olives,
        and Tomato Relish, 128
potatoes, in Breuss Juice Formula, 59

Q

quinoa, 118
    Black Fall Quinoa with Radicchio,
        Shaved Fennel, and Cremini
        Mushrooms, 125
    Broccoli Pesto and Quinoa "Risotto,"
        133
    with Cherries, Olives, Parsley,
        Avocado, and Lemon, 130
    Cinnamon-Scented Quinoa and
        Walnuts, 86
    Coconut Quinoa, 85
    Collard Burrito, 91
Quinoa with Cherries, Olives, Parsley,
    Avocado, and Lemon, 130

R

Radicchio, Shaved Fennel, and Cremini
    Mushrooms, Black Fall Quinoa with,
    125
radishes, in Medicinal Miso, 111
Rainbow Chopped Salad, 107
raisins
    Apple Ginger Water Kefir, 74
    Cardamom Chia Pudding, 85
    Cherry-Pistachio Relish, 98
    Winter Greens and Walnuts, 109
raspberries, in Berry Blend, 51
Raspberry Rhapsody, 27
Red Salad, 105
Rose and Aloe Spritz, 75

S

Salad Spinner, 65
Salt and Sesame Oil Detox Bath, 138
seaweed
    Cauliflower Caviar, 95
    Medicinal Miso, 111
    Millet with Avocado, Sea Vegetables,
        Vegetables, Sesame, and Mint, 127
    Rainbow Chopped Salad, 107
Seaweed Caviar Beet Chip, Avocado
    Crème Fraîche, 96
seeds
    Asian Pear and Avocado Salad, 103
    Cardamom Raisin Pudding, 85
    Carrot Ribbon Pasta with Miso Tahini,
        Shiitakes, and Black Sesame
        Seeds, 129
    Chia and Buckwheat Cereal, 81
    Millet with Avocado, Sea Vegetables,
        Vegetables, Sesame, and Mint, 127
    Shaved Celery Root Linguini,
        Mushrooms, Truffle Pumpkin
        Seeds, and Sage, 121
    White Mushroom Pâté, 97
Shaved Celery Root Linguini, Mushrooms,
    Truffle Pumpkin Seeds, and Sage, 121
Skin Saver, 25
Spice-C, 45
spinach
    Classic, 64
    Curried Spinach Dip, 93
    Glorious Green, 36
    Great Grape, 37
    Magical Melon, 39
    Miso Me-So Green, 39
    Pear-licious, 31
    Pistachio Thyme Pesto, 123
    Tropical Greens, 37

V10, 55
strawberries
    Berry Blend, 51
    Sweet Immunity, 17
Strawberries and Cream Tisane, 76
Summer Heat, 47
Sun-Kissed, 49
Sweet Cream, 61
Sweet Immunity, 17
Sweet Pea "Couscous," with Pistachios,
    Apricots, and Chili, 131
Sweet Pea Hummus, 98
sweet potato, in Sweet Cream, 61
Swiss chard, in Winter Greens and
    Walnuts, 109

T

tahini
    Carrot Ribbon Pasta with Miso Tahini,
        Shiitakes, and Black Sesame
        Seeds, 129
    Millet with Avocado, Sea Vegetables,
        Vegetables, Sesame, and Mint, 127
    Sweet Pea Hummus, 98
tarragon, in Papaya "Poppy," 113
tea
    Chai Mate Latte, 73
    Green Grapefruit, 76
    Matcha Power, 38
    Vanilla Rooibos Tonic, 75
thyme
    Fennel and Grapefruit Salad, 115
    Heart Beet, 62
    Papaya "Poppy," 113
    Pistachio Thyme Pesto, 123
    White Mushroom Pâté, 97
    Winter Greens and Walnuts, 109
tomatillos, in Ceviche Verde, 97

tomatoes
    Collard Burrito, 91
    Mediterranean, 63
    Seed "Caviar," 112
    Relish, 128
    V10, 55
Tropical Greens, 37
Tropical Pop, 27
Tummy Tamer, 25
turmeric
    Blood Orange "Soda," 71
    Carrot Mango Curry Soup, 114
    Heart Beet, 62
    Sweet Cream, 61

V

V10, 55
Vanilla Nut Milk, 83
Vanilla Rooibos Tonic, 75
Vinegar Bath, 137

W

watermelon, in Summer Heat, 47
Watermelon Ice with Avocado Mousse, 87
White Mushroom Pâté, 97
wine, sparkling, in Mimosa Sorbet, 87
Winter Greens and Walnuts, 109

Y

yuzu, in Tropical Pop, 27

Z

zucchini, in Fennel and Zucchini Velouté,
    112
Zucchini Noodles, Pine Nuts, Olives, and
    Tomato Relish, 128

Metric Conversion Chart

Volume Measurements

U.S.	Metric
1 teaspoon	5 ml
1 tablespoon	15 ml
1/4 cup	60 ml
1/3 cup	75 ml
1/2 cup	125 ml
2/3 cup	150 ml
3/4 cup	175 ml
1 cup	250 ml

Weight Measurements

U.S.	Metric
1/2 ounce	15 g
1 ounce	30 g
3 ounces	90 g
4 ounces	115 g
8 ounces	225 g
12 ounces	350 g
1 pound	450 g
2 1/4 pounds	1 kg

Temperature Conversion

Fahrenheit	Celsius
250	120
300	150
325	160
350	180
375	190
400	200
425	220
450	230